MOTTO English

A Communication Booster for Japanese Learners
豊かな人生を楽しむ英会話

AKI TAKANO

SANKEISHA

学習者の皆さんへ

『MOTTO English』ワールドへようこそ！

　このテキストは英会話を学ぶことによって人生を豊かにしたいと願う学習者の皆さんのために作成されたものです。皆さんの会話力を上達させる秘訣を満載しています。

　英会話を趣味にしているあなたは、健康的な生活を送るのにたいへん効果的な選択をしていると言えるでしょう。仲間と会話すること、声を出すこと、高度な思考力を使うこと、物事を学ぶ好奇心を発揮していること、刺激を受けること、外出すること——すべてが認知症予防であり、脳トレであり、精神衛生向上に貢献するものであり、教室の距離によってはエクササイズまで網羅してくれます。

　さらに、英語が話せるメリットはとても大きく、世界中の人と直接意思の疎通ができ、気の合う人とは友人関係を築くこともできる、海外旅行で言葉の苦労がなくなる、英語ができる自分が純粋に嬉しい、そして、少なくとも何人かの身近な人に、尊敬のまなざしで見てもらうことができます。

　英会話学習は、どんなに年齢を重ねてもできるので、生涯の友となりえます。語学は使っていないとさび付いてしまうという、ほうっておかれるのが苦手な趣味でもありますので、長くよいお付き合いをしたいものです。

　本テキストをもっとも効率よく使っていただくために、次ページの「英会話を学ぶ心構え」を心に留めて、レッスンを満喫していただければ幸いです。

　皆さんの英会話力の向上を心から願ってやみません。

髙野　あき

英会話を学ぶ心構え

■ 仲間やティーチャーと学ぶことを楽しもう

　英会話はひとりでは学べません。お互いに相手がいてこそできるのが会話です。あなたの貴重な時間を共有する人たちが、いままさにあなたの人生の中で、共通の趣味を持つ仲間として存在しています。あなたの意見を聞き、共感し、インスパイアし、新たな視点に気づかせてくれるのです。彼らと過ごす時間を大いに楽しみましょう。

■ 時間をかけよう

　会話と自己学習、両方に時間をかけましょう。アウトプットはレッスンで、インプットは自己学習で鍛えます。語学の習熟度は、よく学習にかける時間の量で表されます。外国語を習得して使いこなすのには、それなりの時間がかかりますが、時間をかければ上達します。

■ 継続は力なり

　居心地のよい会話のクラスを選び、とにかく継続することです。ひとりひとり、やりやすいと思う環境ややり方、教材が違います。やるべきこと、やれることを粛々とやります。達成しやすい短期での目標を決めるのもいいでしょう。重ねた努力を振り返ってみることも励みになります。

■ 上達に気づこう

　語学は上達が目に見えないので、自分のスキルが上がっていることはわかりづらいものです。ところが、じつは、大変わかりやすい指標があります。新しい単語に出会った、知っていた単語なのに知らなかった意味が出てきた、初めて知ったイディオムがあった、これらはひとつひとつすべてが、あなたの進歩の証なのです。あなたの学習の範囲が広がり、ステップアップしたからこそ、新たに視野に入ってきた知識なのです。山に登るのと同じですね。この一歩ずつを重ねていきましょう。

■ 英語はいつでもあなたのそばに

　人生にはさまざまなことが起こり、時には好きなことを断念しなくてはいけないときもあるでしょう。その時はきっぱりあきらめましょう。学べる環境が整えば、再開すればいいのです。気楽にいきましょう。英会話は、控えめな、気の長い幼なじみのように、いつもあなたのそばにいるものです。

CONTENTS

本書の使い方

本書は、講師の豊かな語学知識に導かれた英会話学習を想定して作成されています。講師のサポートのもと、クラスの仲間との交流を通してスキルの向上をはかれるよう、各セクションにおいて、学習者の発話へのモチベーションをあげ、会話を発展させる要素を工夫して取り入れています。

対話文

日本語での会話を原文とし、日本人がふだんよく使う言い回しを、英語でどう表現するかを学ぶことを主眼としています。巻末の対訳（p.74～p.77）を参照し、もともとの日本語での脈絡とニュアンスを十分に理解したうえで、会話文の練習ができます。ご自身にとっての「使える表現」をできるだけ多く習得しましょう。

また、ナレーターの音声を正確にリピートすることで、発音、アクセント、全体の抑揚、スピードを訓練することができます。

※下記のURLより、ネイティブの音声データが無料でダウンロードできます。

Build Your Vocabulary

語彙の豊かさは英会話上達の要です。言葉の数を増やすこと、正確な発音を身につけること、脳のメモリに何度もインプットすることを心がけましょう。

Free Talk

与えられたテーマについて、学習した表現や単語を取り入れて、自由に会話を発展させましょう。

Questions

ペアを組んで、またはクラスで、お互いに質問をしてみましょう。コミュニケーションの基本は、相手に興味を持ち、尊重し、情報を与え合うことです。聞かれたことにプラスアルファの情報を加えて相手に伝えると、自然に会話がはずみます。

Imagine

与えられた場面をリアルに思い描いてみて下さい。さあ、あなたはどうするか、相手に伝えたいストーリーが浮かんできますね。話したいことやイメージが頭に浮かんでいることが、会話のもっとも大切な要素です。

Survey

だれがクラスで一番か？など、スコアを競う楽しいパートです。クラスメートの意外な一面を発見するかもしれません。

Exercise

さまざまなアプローチでテーマに関連した知識を深めたり、表現を練習するセクションです。

Expressions

これが使えたら便利、という表現を重点的に練習しましょう。もどかしさが解消され、会話をスムーズに運べるようになります。

Let's Discuss

日本人は、意見を聞かれた時に、賛成なのに反対の立場のメリットに触れたり、あるいは、両方の立場を擁護してしまい、外国の方が混乱することがあります。立場を一方に決め、根拠や例をあげることで、明快な説明をする練習をしてみましょう。

Grammar Tips

多くの学習者が戸惑う文法的なポイントをわかりやすく説明しています。正しい文法に基づいた表現は、会話の質の良さにつながり、相手にとっても理解しやすいものになります。

■音声ダウンロード■

https://www.happyglobeenglish.com/text-audio/　　　キーコード：**MOTTO**

Unit 1 / Gardening

Jun has a garden in the suburbs, rich with greenery. Today, Daniel, the husband of her younger sister Kei, is visiting her. Listen to their conversation and practice with a partner.

Daniel : Jun, your garden is so lovely. Having some tea on the terrace is a real treat for me.

Jun : Tee-hee. It's such precious time, for sure. You came at the perfect time, too, as the flowers in the garden are in full bloom.

Daniel : What are those purple flowers?

Jun : Those are anchusas. Remember I told you I had visited flower gardens in Hokkaido last year? I bought the seeds at the shop in a garden in Furano, and now, look, they've grown into so many blooms!

Daniel : I'd like to have some, too! Could you spare me some seeds when you get them?

Jun : Why not. Can you see the young green of the smoke tree, doesn't it give a lovely touch? I took such care propagating it.

Daniel : Oh, I know, it turns to coral red in the autumn.

Jun : Daniel, I've been thinking of visiting the U.K., which is the cradle of garden culture. Would you two like to join me?

Daniel : Sounds great! Roses are in season around June or July. I'll ask Kei.

Jun : Let's enjoy travelling, sight-seeing and eating the local delicacies, for as long as we're still able to!

Daniel : Ha-ha-ha! You're right. Can you check if there are any tours?

Jun : Okay. I'll take a look, they usually send me a bunch of travel brochures.

Build Your Vocabulary

Match each flower / vegetable name in the boxes below to its Japanese equivalent and write it in. Then, read out the name of each plant.

1. Flowers

向日葵	紫陽花	百合	水仙	朝顔
_____	_____	_____	_____	_____

蘭	菊	秋桜	シクラメン	椿
_____	_____	_____	_____	_____

cosmos / sunflower / lily / hydrangea / cyclamen
orchid / chrysanthemum / daffodil / camellia / morning glory

2. Vegetables

キャベツ	レタス	きゅうり	ほうれん草	なす
_____	_____	_____	_____	_____

ネギ	玉ねぎ	にら	大根	里芋
_____	_____	_____	_____	_____

cucumber / Japanese radish / cabbage / spinach / onion
lettuce / Chinese chive / taro / eggplant / green onion

Free Talk

A. Match the Japanese phrase with the relevant English words, then say them out loud.

じょうろで/植物に/水をやる ● ● till ● ● a hole ● ● with a hoe

くわで/畑を/耕す ● ● water ● ● the plants ● ● with a shovel

スコップで/穴を/掘る ● ● dig ● ● a field ● ● with a watering can

鎌で/庭の/草取りをする ● ● harvest ● ● strawberries ● ● with a net

ハサミで/ナスを/収穫する ● ● weed ● ● an eggplant ● ● with scissors

イチゴに/ネットを/かける ● ● cover ● ● a garden ● ● with a sickle

サヤエンドウに/支柱を/立てる ● ● spray ● ● a snow pea plant ● ● to squash

薔薇に/殺菌剤を/散布する ● ● apply ● ● roses ● ● with supports

カボチャに/肥料を/施す ● ● prop up ● ● fertilizer ● ● with fungicide

B. Do you grow flowers or vegetables? Use the phrases above to talk about your own gardening work, making complete sentences.

Questions

Work together with your partner. Take turns to ask each other the questions given below. Try to give some extra information related to the question.

1. Which do you prefer growing, flowers or vegetables?
2. How long do you spend working with plants in a day or in a week?
3. Do you think you have green fingers?
4. What flower do you think is the most difficult to take care of?
5. What vegetable do you think is the easiest to grow?
6. What's the best or most fun part about growing plants yourself?
7. Are there any popular flower gardens in your area?
8. Have you visited any famous flower gardens in Japan or abroad?

Imagine

Imagine you were suddenly given a great big piece of land at the foot of Mt. Fuji. What would you do? Choose one from options a-e below. Then, add a few sentences to describe your imaginary life there.

1. Build a wonderful villa with a garden for your family and guests.
2. Cultivate the land to plant highland vegetables.
3. Run a great vineyard.
4. Turn it into pasture and keep sheep, goats and cows.
5. Level the ground and set up courses for horse riding. And of course, keep some horses in a barn there!

While working in his office, Hiroshi hears the door open and sees a foreign person standing there with a worried expression. Listen to their conversation and practice with a partner.

Girl : Hi, can you speak English?

Hiroshi : Yes, what's happened? Is something wrong?

Girl : Oh, thank goodness! I'm looking for a bank, is there one near here?

Hiroshi : Will any bank do? You need to draw money from an ATM, right?

Girl : That's right.

Hiroshi : Okay, there are a couple nearby. Go out the door, make a right. You'll see the convenience store.

Girl : Let me see… Oh, yes, I see it.

Hiroshi : Turn right at the traffic signals there, then at the next signals you make a left, and soon you'll see a NICE Shinkin Bank on your left. There's a Cherry Bank nearby it as well, just ahead, at the corner on the same block.

Girl : Can I just check that again please? At those signals, I turn to the right, at the next signals I turn to the left, is that right?

Hiroshi : That's right.

Girl : Thank you. That's helped a lot. I asked some other people but couldn't make myself understood.

Hiroshi : Glad I could be of help. Take care.

Girl : Thanks! Have a good day!

Build Your Vocabulary

What landmarks are there in your neighborhood which you can give directions for? Match the words.

交差点 ●	● bus stop	一区画 ●	● pedestrian crossing
踏切 ●	● intersection	つきあたり ●	● side walk
地下鉄出入口 ●	● subway exit	横断歩道 ●	● block
バス停 ●	● railroad crossing	歩道 ●	● National Route 16
看板・標識 ●	● sign	国道16号線 ●	● the end of the road
弁当屋 ●	● gas station	警察署 ●	● police station
ショッピングセンター ●	● video arcade	交番 ●	● fire station
ゲームセンター ●	● hair salon	消防署 ●	● city hall
美容院 ●	● lunch box store	市役所 ●	● community center
ガソリンスタンド ●	● shopping mall	公民館 ●	● police box

Exercise
Explain how to get there

Look at the map and explain how to get to your destination. Fill in the blanks using words chosen from the box below each paragraph.

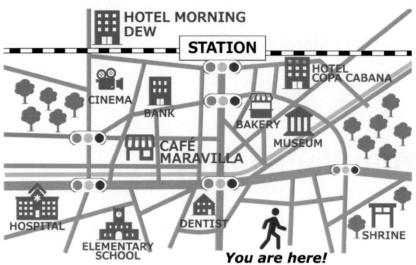

1. Café Maravilla

To get to the Café Maravilla, you _____, turn left at the _____ of the road, _____ the signal, and take the _____ narrow street on your right, then turn left _____ the first corner. You will _____ the cafeteria _____ .

> cross / second / go straight / end / at / on your right / see

2. Hotel Morning Dew

To get to the Hotel Morning Dew, go straight, then _____ at the end of the road. Turn right at the second _____ and _____ . Walk past _____ the cinema, then cross at the _____ . The hotel is on your right.

> railroad crossing / turn left / keep walking / intersection / the front of

Free Talk

Work with a partner. Think of the closest **convenience store**, **supermarket**, **ATM** and **place to eat** from your class. Role play by asking and answering directions to get to each location.

A : I think I need to buy some lunch today.

B : There is a convenience store near here. You go left, walk two blocks, …

Survey

The King / Queen of Poor Sense of Direction!

Answer the questions. For "Yes / No" answers, circle the score in the frame. The student who gets the highest points is the king/queen!

	Question	Yes	No
1	Have you ever got lost when you visited some place for the first time?	1	0
2	Have you ever ended up right back where you started?	3	0
3	Is it easier for you to find where you are by turning the map so that your destination is at the top?	2	0
4	Do you always rely on the GPS even for places familiar to you?	3	0
5	Can you tell East from West and North from South correctly?	-1	2
6	You tend to start walking in the wrong direction as soon as you leave shops or restaurants.	2	0
7	Sometimes you cannot find your way back to your hotel room. *Tip: Be careful in answering this. Your answer should be "no" if this tends to happen to you.*	0	3
8	Have your friends ever said to you, "Hey, not that way. Where are you heading?"	2	0
9	Do you find yourself disoriented when you turn a corner and then immediately turn another one?	3	0
10	Have you ever taken the wrong train and ended up going in the opposite direction?	2	0
	Score		
	Sum Total		

If you do find out you have a terrible sense of direction, don't worry! You have sharp eyes, a tongue in your mouth, and all the communication skills you need to find your destination!
Also, in this class, you might just have found someone with a better sense of direction! Take them with you!

Unit 3 / Gastronomy

Teru and Kazuo have been close friends in English class for years. Being a foody, Kazuo has become a local food guide. Listen to their conversation and practice with a partner.

Teru : Hey, what's 'gastronomy'? I mean, I learnt that the city of Tsuruoka has joined UNESCO's creative cities network, in the field of gastronomy.

Kazuo : Well, gastronomy is often used to mean gourmet, but it can be used for a wide range of aspects related to food.

Teru : I don't quite understand. Could you please break it down for me?

Kazuo : Sure, it's not just about the food itself, it's also about how traditional dishes are rooted in the local area, local eating habits, the way that foods are fished and farmed, even the ecosystem or 'terroir' of a place.

Teru : If that's so, it can relate to many aspects!

Kazuo : If we look closely at any field of gastronomy, we can sometimes see that our culture, which we usually take for granted, is quite unique when looked at from a global perspective. For instance, one of the characteristics of our food culture is wild gastronomy.

Teru : Wild? It sounds like we are eating some pretty dreadful food, doesn't it?

Kazuo : Ha-ha. Yeah, it does. We Japanese often pick wild vegetables in the mountains and fields, other than the crops we grow. We also eat wild animals.

Teru : Speaking of which, I hear eating seaweed is also fairly rare across world cultures.

Kazuo : It's healthy, and low in calories. Nowadays people all over the world are increasingly health-conscious, and seaweed is attracting attention as the perfect food to meet their needs. We even have insect-based dishes, like bee larvae and locusts.

Teru : I know! Some researchers say eating insects is one of the most viable sources of protein. I'd rather not try though!

Kazuo : When I was in elementary school, the whole class used to go to the rice fields to catch locusts during school hours. There are still schools which serve locusts cooked in sweetened soy source, called *tsukudani*, for lunch.

Teru : Do they? Oh, that must be...interesting...

Build Your Vocabulary

Match the words, then say them out loud.

昆虫食 •　　• Shojin ryori　　　　山菜 •　　• mountain vegetables

分子料理 •　　• molecular cuisine　　地産地消 •　　• fermented food

精進料理 •　　• eating insects　　　発酵食品 •　　• foodie

海藻食 •　　• eating seaweed　　食べ歩き好き •　　• local production and consumption

Questions　　Work in pairs, taking turns to ask and answer the questions below.

Mountain vegetables
1. How many mountain vegetables do you know? Name them.
2. What's your most favorite mountain vegetable dish?
3. Have you ever picked mountain vegetables?

Insects
1. Do you have any special memories of eating insects?
2. Do you think that you will be eating insects on a daily basis in the future?

Expressions

In English conversations, euphemistic expressions are often used. When Japanese people talk in English, they may sometimes sound rude. Here are some tips to soften your language.

Case 1 "I don't know", "I'm not sure"

A : I think that plan A is a good idea.

B : I don't think so.

A : Oh...

→

A : I think that plan A is a good idea.

B : I... don't know. How about taking a look at plan B?

A : Hmm, OK, let's.

A : A is a good restaurant.

B : I don't like it.

A : Oh...

→

A : A is a good restaurant.

B : I'm not so sure. I'd rather eat at B.

A : Oh, would you?

Case 2 "I wish I could", "Unfortunately", "I'm afraid"

A : Let's have a barbecue tomorrow!

B : No, I can't. Sorry, I'm busy.

A : Oh-oh...

→

A : Let's have a barbecue tomorrow!

B : I wish I could. Unfortunately, I already have plans with my family.

A : OK, maybe next time.

A : Why don't we reserve seats for this Friday?

B : I can't.

A : Oh-oh...

→

A : Why don't we reserve seats for this Friday?

B : I'm afraid I can't make it. My schedule is too tight. How about next week?

A : Sure. I'll call to make a reservation.

Now make pairs. Think of a plan to do something this weekend. Partner A suggests a plan and Partner B turns down the idea using 'softer' / 'less direct' language.

Let's Discuss

Fast Food vs Slow Food

Work in groups. Group A supports fast food and Group B supports slow food. First, talk about the merits / disadvantages of each food style in the group, then discuss and try to convince the other side. Allow everyone to have time to speak, then switch roles.

Here are some clues. Add your own ideas.

eco-friendly   served quickly   provides jobs for local people

supports local farmers   low cost   cheap

Questions

Answer the questions below, share information with the class.

Eating places in your area

1. Are there any good restaurants in your town to recommend to foreign tourists?
2. Which restaurant / izakaya bar / coffee house would you take your Japanese foodie friends to when they've travelled a long way to visit you?
3. Are there any restaurants or izakaya bars where you can enjoy relaxing with your close friends?

Good restaurants

1. Have you ever had lunch or dinner at a Michelin-starred restaurant? Where was it?
2. Which eating place is the best you've ever been to?
3. What makes a good restaurant?

Good producers / farming experiences

1. What special agricultural foodstuffs are produced in your area?
2. Do you know any good food producers in your area?
3. Have you ever joined in any farming work experiences or tours?
4. Have you ever stayed at farmhouse accommodation? If so, what was it like?

Shojin ryori

1. How often do you eat Shojin ryori?
2. Do you know where we can have Shojin ryori?
3. What's the difference between Shojin ryori and vegetarian food?

Tips for Building Vocabulary

Do you forget words easily? Don't worry, your memory is functioning quite normally! Relax! Many people struggle to memorize English words, saying "I just can't get them into my head!" Perhaps some of us misunderstand how memory works, so here are some helpful tips for memorizing words.

1. Relax. No need to memorize.

- Let your brain chew over the words at least once.
- Allow your memory to forget the words after this process.

2. Encounter new words, as many as you can.

As you keep studying, you will encounter lots of different words. When the same words appear in your learning materials repeatedly, your brain will recognize them as important and worthy of retaining in your memory. Some researchers say this process occurs after you have spotted a word between four to eleven times.

3. Try to correctly pronounce the new words five times.

To use a word, you need to know the correct sound, meaning, and hopefully the spelling. When these three factors are put together, you will be able to use it. Try to pronounce the word aloud until you are sure you are pronouncing it correctly and smoothly. Saying the word out loud will also help the brain to acquire it through the sense of hearing.

For any words you're not sure how to pronounce, ask your teacher for help!

4. For long or difficult words, break them into word parts.

Some words are difficult to pronounce. Break them into word parts; prefixes（接頭語）, roots（語幹）and suffixes（接尾語）. Then practice each word aloud five times.

e.g. extraordinary → extra / ordinary
  indispensable → in / dispensa / ble
  acrophobia → acro / phobia

Let's take a survey!

Study hours

1. How many hours do you study English a week?
2. How many hours do you study monthly and yearly?
3. How many hours have you studied since you started learning English as an adult?
4. Let's say our first target for acquiring good, basic English skills is 1,000 hours. When will you hit the 1,000 hours target? Or have you already met it? If you've met this target already, you can be proud of yourself, "I speak English well!"

Vocabulary

1. How many new words do you learn in a lesson and period of self-study?
2. Calculate the number of new words you acquire monthly and yearly.
3. Multiply the number of words you learn yearly with the years you have studied.
4. How much have you improved your vocabulary since you started to learn English as an adult?
5. Let's say our target number of words to acquire is 2,600. When will you meet this target? Or, have you already done so?

Share Information with Your Classmate

Do you have any tips to improve conversation skills? Do you have any materials or TV/radio programs to recommend to your friends to learn English? Talk with the class.

Unit 4 Viewing the Blossoms

Yoko and Takashi work within the same department of a company in Osaka. Takashi is popular as a manager among subordinates because he cares for his staff very much. Listen to their conversation and practice with a partner.

Yoko : Wow, it's in full bloom! We're so lucky we've come at the best time. Viewing the cherry blossoms at the Mint on a clear night is very special!

Takashi : Absolutely! Most of the trees are double-blossom varieties, and their blossoms tend to be a beautiful deep pink. After enjoying the somei-yoshino variety, we can appreciate the different charms of other cherry blossoms.

Yoko : This variety is beni-temari, which means red balls. Look at the tip of this branch, so many balls of blossoms. Whoa, this lovely fragrance. This old stately tree is Yang Guifei. What a fascinating name!

Takashi : Oh, boy. Kacho is walking fast, he is a man in a hurry. I guess he's thinking only of the drinking party.

Yoko : Of course he is! He started looking impatient from noon, he even knocked off from his job earlier than usual.

Takashi : We all came together, but he has his head in the clouds! We're here to admire the flowers, right?

Yoko : Easy, boss, we know this place very well in the department, we're here every year, regular as clockwork! In fact, we have a saying, "Dumplings are better than cherry blossoms". Plus, as manager, when you're with us, we can go to places we usually cannot go to!

Takashi : You know what? It's always me that ends up treating you all. My wallet gets sick after drinking parties.

Yoko : Your good point is your generosity. If your people feel good, you'll feel good. Nobody will ever say 'No' to you when you ask us to do something!

Takashi : Is that so? Wait, you said "That's not my job" when I asked you to do something this morning!

Yoko : Did I?

Questions

Do you love cherry blossoms? Work in pairs to ask and answer the questions below.

1. Name some famous places for cherry blossoms in Japan.
2. Where in Japan, that you have visited, is the best place for viewing cherry blossoms?
3. Are there any good places to enjoy cherry blossoms in your neighborhood? Where would you recommend your classmates to visit?
4. Have you ever had parties outside with your family, friends, or colleagues during cherry blossom season?
5. What's your favorite way to view cherry blossoms?
6. Do you have any unforgettable memories related to cherry blossoms?

Build Your Vocabulary

Circle those adjectives which can be used as alternatives to the section in a frame, without significantly changing the meaning of the sentence.

Wow, the cherry flowers here are | so beautiful | !

| fantastic | superb | curious | brilliant | marvelous | great |

| lovely | odd | gorgeous | strange | wonderful | terrific |

| horrible | miserable | impeccable | amazing |

| impressive | excellent | unusual | inspiring |

| annoying | splendid | spectacular | hilarious |

| attractive | good-looking |

Let's Discuss Recently, popular flower viewing sites are attracting more and more people. Discuss the issues below with your classmates.

1. What are the merits of attracting many visitors to flower viewing sites?
2. How can we attract more visitors to the scenic spots or attractions in our area?
3. What are the problems with popular flower viewing spots? Are there any sites with such problems in your neighborhood?
4. Do you have any good ideas to help cope with the problems discussed above, to ensure that both locals and visitors can happily enjoy the flowers when they are in season?

Exercise
Guess what?

Flower fairs often include stalls. Many people enjoy walking around attractions and eating street food. Here are many types of stalls. Guess what type of stall they are and write down the corresponding letter in the box on the right.

1. It's a popular Japanese style pancake. It contains eggs, sliced cabbage, sliced pork, etc., topped with dried bonito shavings and green laver.

2. You try to catch live goldfish in the water using a paper scoop called a 'poi'. As the paper is thin, when the poi touches water, it is easily broken. It's difficult to scoop even a single fish. That's what makes it such fun!

3. You shoot targets with a toy gun to win prizes such as snacks, stuffed animals, toys, etc. To get the prize, your bullet needs to hit the prize so that the prize falls to the floor.

4. You pick a slip from a basket. If your slip has a winning number, you get the corresponding prize, though sometimes the slip just has "won" on it.

5. You toss some rings to try to target the prize you want, such as toys, snacks, etc. The rules are usually pretty tough, your ring must land around the prize and drop onto the shelf, without making the item fall.

6. It's a very popular sweet sold at fairs, made of granulated sugar and looks like a little cloud.

A. Shooting Gallery   **B.** Okonomiyaki   **C.** Lottery
D. Ring Toss   **E.** Cotton Candy   **F.** Goldfish Scooping

Unit 5 / My False Tooth Came Out!

Marie and Joe are close friends in English class. Today, when Marie came to the class, Joe noticed that something wasn't quite right. Listen to their conversation and practice with a partner.

Marie : Hi, there!

Joe : Oh, Marie, what happened to your front tooth?!

Marie : Ha-ha-ha! My front false tooth came out.

Joe : It happened to me, too, a few years back.

Marie : Really?

Joe : Yeah, it was during my visit to Canada. I was having a fantastic lunch, actually biting into a magnificent lobster, then it just fell out.

Marie : A-ha-ha! And where did the tooth go?

Joe : Onto my stomach!

Marie : Gee, that must have been troublesome!

Joe : Tee-hee, not really. I hid the gap with my upper lip and tried to smile with my mouth open just a little. Nobody noticed!

Joe & Marie : Ha-ha-ha!

Joe : And, what were you eating when your tooth came out?

Marie : It was Moso bamboo soup. I didn't even notice that I'd lost it. While

watching TV, my husband suddenly said, 'hey your tooth is missing'.

Joe   : So, the Moso bamboo took your tooth. No wonder, it's quite chewy in texture.

Marie   : You know, teeth are expensive. But if you take the tooth that's fallen out to the dentist, they can use it again, you don't have to pay very much.

Joe   : Then let's be careful with bamboo shoots and lobsters!

Joe & Marie : Ha-ha-ha!

Build Your Vocabulary

Match the words, then say them out loud.

親知らず ●	● tooth decay	上の / 下の歯 ●	● gum
前 / 奥歯 ●	● tooth ache	入れ歯 / さし歯 ●	● false tooth / teeth
虫歯 ●	● hypersensitivity	歯茎 ●	● upper / lower teeth
歯痛 ●	● wisdom tooth	歯周病 ●	● bad breath
知覚過敏 ●	● front / back tooth	口臭 ●	● periodontal disease
近眼 ●	● longsighted	目薬 ●	● floaters
老眼 ●	● reading glasses	疲れ目 ●	● cataract
老眼鏡 ●	● bloodshot eyes	白内障 ●	● eyestrain
目の充血 ●	● astigmatism	緑内障 ●	● glaucoma
乱視 ●	● shortsighted	飛蚊症 ●	● eye drops

Grammar Tips

Irregular nouns - Singular / Plural

Singular and plural of nouns can often be confusing! Let's check out some of them!

Different form		
foot - feet	mouse - mice	wolf - wolves
tooth - teeth	child - children	leaf - leaves
goose - geese	man - men	life - lives
die - dice	woman - women	half - halves

Same form		
fish	carp	series
salmon	sheep	aircraft
trout	cattle	species
shellfish	deer	Japanese

A. Circle the correct forms.

1. My (foot / feet) are cold. My right (foot / feet) hurts.
2. I saw several (child / children) playing soccer in the stadium.
3. My (tooth / teeth) came out, so I took it to the dentist.
4. (Wolf / Wolves) live in a pack.
5. Autumn (leaf / leaves) glitter in the morning sun.
6. We enjoy our (life / lives) together.
7. Two (half / halves) make a whole loaf of bread.

B. Fill in the blanks.

1. The book consists of four _____ (シリーズ).
2. The fisherman caught a couple of _____ (鮭) that day.
3. I'm allergic to _____ (貝類・甲殻類).
4. We see many _____ (鯉) swimming in the moat.
5. There are _____ (羊) and _____ (牛) eating grass in the meadow.
6. A large number of animal _____ (種) are in danger of extinction.
7. Most _____ (日本人) are familiar with foreign cuisines.

Exercise
Think about it!

Dental Implants

Recently, dental implants have become popular. Here are some advantages and disadvantages of dental implants. Please sort the sentences below into advantages and disadvantages.

Advantages (   ) (   ) (   ) (   )

Disadvantages (   ) (   ) (   ) (   )

1. Gives a natural looking equivalent to your original teeth.
2. Initial cost is expensive, and it's not covered by insurance.
3. Requires maintenance.
4. Lasts longer than other procedures, such as bridgework or dentures.
5. No need to pare down other healthy teeth.
6. Requires replacement of the crowns.
7. Risks of swelling and pain after surgery.
8. Gives the same bite strength as natural teeth.

Questions

Answer the following questions. When answering "Yes / No", add some extra information such as when, how, where, why, etc. Please remember though, your story should be finished within three minutes, to allow other classmates to share their stories!

Teeth
1. Have you ever had a tooth or false tooth come out, other than milk teeth?
2. Have you had your wisdom teeth pulled out?
3. What's the worst memory you have relating to oral health?
4. How do you keep your gums and teeth healthy?
5. What food do you think is worst for your teeth?

Eyes
1. Are you short-sighted, or long-sighted?
2. Do you wear glasses, including fashion items?
3. Have you or your parents suffered from cataracts?
4. Are you trying any special treatments or supplements to maintain your vision?
5. Do you get eyestrain from any of your daily activities?

Unit 6 Silly Me!

Miki and Dai are close cousins. They love traveling abroad and this year they have been visiting their favorite destination, Hawaii. Listen to their conversation and practice with a partner.

Miki : Oh my gosh! Seems like I left all the air tickets at the hotel!

Dai : What!?! Seriously? Calm down and check carefully.

Miki : I don't think I put them in my bag. I checked the flight schedule at the table this morning and left the file there. The tickets from Kona to Honolulu and Honolulu to Haneda are all in the file.

Dai : Let's call the hotel immediately.

Miki : Sure... Where is my cell phone? Oh, no... my cell phone is gone!

Dai : Miki, easy, don't be upset. I'm sure you'll have it. Look for it carefully.

Miki : Okay, I will, need to chill out, right? Oh yes! Here it is.

Miki : It's such a shame, we're only two kilometers from the coffee farm, and we have to return to the hotel. How come I'm this absentminded?

Dai : Take it easy. It happens to everybody. We were fortunate as the Hotel kept our tickets. What if they had thrown them away...?

Miki : I had wanted to visit the coffee farm. It was recommended by some locals, so it should be a good farm. I was thinking of getting some souvenirs there.

28

Dai   : There are loads of places we haven't visited yet, so why don't we come back again next year? On you.

Miki   : On me? Seriously?

Dai   : I am, yeah.

Build Your Vocabulary

Here are some terms to describe personality traits. Match the words, then say them out loud.

あわてんぼう •	• easy going	温厚 •	• mild
ぼんやりさん •	• a worrier	世話好き •	• outgoing
のんびり屋 •	• absent-minded	頑張りや •	• positive
短気 •	• short-tempered	礼儀正しい •	• caring
石頭 •	• hasty	負けず嫌い •	• diligent
不器用 •	• stubborn	前向き •	• a sore looser
心配性 •	• a klutz	社交的 •	• polite

Exercise
Describe Yourself and the People around You

Are you an easy going or hasty person? Describe your characteristics, and those of your family, friends, colleagues, etc., by using the model sentence below. Try to make more than two sentences for each person.

> I think I'm pretty easy going. I'd say, I do things at my own pace and rarely get upset.
> But my father, he is a big worrier. He is always worried about what I do, where I go, who I'm with...

Grammar Tips

Irregular verbs

Here are some commonly used verbs. Fill in each blank with the past participle. Read aloud to make sure your pronunciation is correct.

read	–	read	– ( )	catch	–	caught	– ( )
shut	–	shut	– ( )	write	–	wrote	– ( )
quit	–	quit	– ( )	wear	–	wore	– ( )
spend	–	spent	– ( )	choose	–	chose	– ( )
buy	–	bought	– ( )	forget	–	forgot	– ( )
sleep	–	slept	– ( )	forgive	–	forgave	– ( )
bring	–	brought	– ( )	fly	–	flew	– ( )

Expressions

"I should have...", "I shouldn't have..."

When you regret what you didn't do, or what you have done, here are some helpful expressions.

Make sentences using the verbs below. In order to become familiar with the usage, recite them from memory. Add your own ideas, too.

Example 1 : I should have checked the room before I left.

tell the truth	work harder	consult with a professional

sleep earlier	set an alarm	your idea

Example 2 : I shouldn't have bought the bag.

tell lies	quit the job	break my word

spend so much money	oversleep	your idea

Questions

Work with a partner. Take turns asking and answering the questions. When answering, give your partner some extra information related to the question.

Mistakes

1. Have you ever lost any tickets for travel or important events?
2. Have you ever lost your wallet somewhere and never got it back?
3. Have you ever missed a flight, train or bus you had booked?
4. What is the most annoying mistake you've made in the past?
5. What is the funniest mistake you've ever made?
6. What is the funniest mistake you've seen someone else make?

Travel

1. Which do you prefer, travelling as part of a package tour group, or making travel plans by yourself?
2. Of the countries you've been to, which is your favorite?
3. What attractions in your favorite country would you recommend to your classmates?
4. Which would be your dream country to visit in the future?
5. For your next trip, which would you prefer – to go on a cruise ship holiday, to fly to your holiday destination, or to take a bus tour?

Describing People

Scene A

Lots of friends are spending time outdoors! Take turns to tell the class what they are doing.

Scene B

Lots of friends are spending time indoors! Take turns to tell the class what they are doing.

Unit 7 / Cooking

One of the attractions for foodies visiting the Basque Country is cooking classes hosted by local chefs, featuring traditional Spanish dishes. Listen to the conversation between the host chef Markel and a participant Julia, then practice with a partner.

Markel : Ojos, everybody! Today we're going to make two types of paella. Seafood paella is well known across the world, but each area has its own flavors according to its local ingredients and recipes. Meat paella is also delicious, so please do enjoy both of them today.

Julia : Look at these gorgeous scampis! And these are mussels and squid, right?

Markel : Aha. The meat is chicken. All ingredients are fresh and sourced locally. We Basque people have a strong preference for local produce.

Julia : In our country, we also have the phrase "locally produced, locally consumed", which basically means, let's eat local produce.

Markel : Then have you heard the phrase "kilometro zero"? That means, from the farmer to the kitchen, the distance is very short, within a zero-kilometer range. By using ingredients from local farmland, consumers can eat fresh food, which also supports and protects local producers. This also helps to reduce the fuel used to transport foods which helps to cut CO_2 emissions.

Julia : Cool. I guess people all over the world who care seriously about their food culture have similar ideas.

Markel : Bueno, the prawns are eagerly waiting for us to get stuck in. Slice the garlic and chop the tomatoes. Put the paella pan on a medium heat, and fry them.

Julia : The stock is hot enough, Markel. Can I put saffron in here?

Markel : Okay, go ahead, it's five minutes to infuse the stock. When the tomato in the pan becomes paste-like in texture, put the bomba rice in it and pour in the stock.

Julia : Now we need to be careful about the heat. High for the first five minutes, then low for ten minutes, then we place the seafood on top of the rice, and on a high heat again.

Markel : Excellent! Julia, you're very welcome as my assistant! When the rice is tender, it's ready. Now why don't we enjoy a chat while we wait for the rice to be cooked, and savour this fantastic Chacoli wine!

Julia : Hooray, I'm in!

Build Your Vocabulary

Match the words, then say them out loud.

野菜の煮物 ● ● Western cuisine   バイキング ● ● noodle

鍋物 ● ● a bowl of beef over rice   バーベキュー ● ● grilled fish

天ぷら ● ● hot pot   焼き魚 ● ● buffet

洋食 ● ● simmered vegetables   オーブン料理 ● ● vegetable with sesame dressing

刺身 ● ● deep fried dish   麺 ● ● grilled dish

寿司 ● ● raw fish   野菜の胡麻和え ● ● oven dish

牛丼 ● ● sushi   大根の甘酢和え ● ● Japanese radish dressed with sweetened vinegar

Exercise
Cooking Methods

Sometimes we need to explain food to friends from foreign countries. Cooking terms are very useful in explaining what the dish is like. Fill in the blanks with words from the frame below, if necessary changing them into their appropriate forms.

steam / simmer / boil / stir-fry / grill / deep-fry / bake
ferment / pan fry (sauté) / cool / roast / freeze / sear

1. To make tempura, we _____ the ingredients.
2. Crabs are generally _____ and _____ when sold at supermarkets.
3. To cook the perfect steak, we _____ the beef cut to get a crispy crust outside.
4. For "*nimono*", we _____ the ingredients with dashi, mirin and soy source.
5. For "*yasai-itame*", we _____ vegetables which have been Julienne cut.
6. To make "*yakitori*", we _____ chicken on skewers.
7. Making yogurt is simple; you stir the starter culture into _____ milk, and let it _____ naturally.
8. We _____ the dough in an oven when making bread.
9. I treat my friends to my handmade _____ pork buns. We call them "*nikuman*".

Questions

Work with a partner. Take turns asking and answering the questions. When answering, give your partner some extra information related to the question.

1. How often do you cook?
2. What are your favorite ingredients for miso soup?
3. What food would you least like to cook or prepare?
4. What's your favorite dish for spoiling your guests?
5. Have you ever attended any cooking class other than home economics at school?
6. Do you know any great chefs personally?

Exercise
Explain the Dish

Work with a partner to name a couple of traditional dishes from your area. Then, tell the class how to prepare those dishes including tips to make them really delicious. Use the table to prepare your explanation.

Name of Dish	Ingredients	Cooking methods	Tips

Unit 8 Health

Marina and Eiji are close friends in an English class. Listen to their conversation and practice with a partner.

Eiji : I had a complete physical yesterday, and I hated the stomach camera.

Marina : I don't like it either. It was so horrible the other time that, when I had to have it again, I chose to take the camera through the nose instead.

Eiji : Have you had your checkup already? I have it in my birth month, every year.

Marina : I had it last month, got the results already, but they didn't come back clear. I've got high blood pressure, my blood sugar is not good, and my cholesterol isn't good either.

Eiji : That's not good. You are on the fast track to ill-health! Doesn't the results sheet say you need further tests?

Marina : Yes, it does. What I'm most worried about is the kidney function. Yesterday I brought the sheet to my home doctor, he recommended that I go to a specialized hospital, and wrote a letter of introduction.

Eiji : Too bad. You'd better start the treatment quickly, or things will get serious.

Marina : Recently I've started getting tired easily and I feel heavy. I'm sleepy all

day. And to top it all off, I have stomach inflammation, too!

Eiji : You have stomach inflammation? Maybe you are eating too much!

Marina : Oh, well, actually I have a good appetite.

Eiji : See? It's good for you that you can eat, anyway. People who eat a lot are full of vitality.

Marina : Eating is one of the pleasures in life. I'm going to die from stress if I can't have cake!

Eiji : Wait, wait. The cakes are the reason for the bad cholesterol, aren't they? You need to care about what you eat as you have a problem with cholesterol. Blue back fish and olive oil would help improve it, right?

Marina : Dietary fiber, too. I definitely need to control my diet so that I can keep eating cakes forever!

Build Your Vocabulary

Match the words, then say them out loud. Medical terms are generally difficult to pronounce. Ask your teacher for help or consult with your dictionary or dictionary device.

身体測定 ●   ● blood pressure   腹部超音波 ●   ● abdominal ultrasound

血圧 ●   ● electrocardiogram   血液検査 ●   ● urine test

心電図 ●   ● physical measurement   尿検査 ●   ● blood test

視力 ●   ● respiratory function   便検査 ●   ● physical examination

聴力 ●   ● audiometry   内科検診 ●   ● breast cancer screening

呼吸機能 ●   ● visual acuity   乳がん検診 ●   ● stool test

胸部X線 ●   ● upper gastrointestinal X-ray   婦人科検診 ●   ● prostate examination

消化管X線 ●   ● chest X ray   前立腺 ●   ● hepatitis C

消化管内視鏡 ●   ● upper gastrointestinal endoscopy   C型肝炎 ●   ● gynecological examination

Questions

Work with a partner. Ask and answer the questions in turn. When answering, add some extra information related to the question.

1. Do you get a complete physical checkup regularly? Where do you get it?
2. What are the merits of having a physical checkup?
3. What kind of physical exam do you hate the most?
4. Which doctor in your area is good at large intestine endoscopy?
5. Where do you get flu vaccinations?

Expressions   <need to + verb> vs <have to+ verb>

Let's make sure we have a clear understanding of the difference between <need to + verb> and <have to + verb> when talking about responsibility.

need to + verb : For cases where **you** feel it is important or necessary to do something; e.g. "I need to improve my English skills to fully enjoy my trip abroad".

have to + verb : For cases where there are **external factors** which require you to do something, e.g. "I have to improve my English skills to get a promotion".

Here are some common errands we do in everyday life. Make sentences using either of the two expressions above. The usage would vary depending on the situation.

get a health checkup	wash the car	celebrate the birthday of a close friend
do dishes buy some food	go to a bank	make dinner go to a drug store
take care of the family	check emails	pay bills take care of the garden
do laundry ask friends to eat out	do homework	clean the house

Survey

Are you leading a healthy life? Here is a survey on habits which are supposed to contribute to physical and mental wellness. Place tags in the column. Who in the class has the healthiest lifestyle?

1	Do you get enough sleep?	
2	Do you make space for quiet time and relaxation in daily life?	
3	Do you get enough sunlight?	
4	Do you engage in aerobic exercise regularly?	
5	Do you engage in anaerobic exercise regularly?	
6	Do you try to cut down on oily foods?	
7	Do you enjoy eating fruits and vegetables?	
8	Do you limit how much alcohol you drink?	
9	Do you try to reduce your salt and sugar intake?	
10	Do you eat regularly and control your portion sizes?	
11	Do you drink plenty of water?	
12	Do you maintain a healthy weight?	
13	Do you enjoy socializing?	
14	Do you make time for your hobbies or favorite projects?	
15	Are you surrounded by good people?	
	Score	

Unit 9 / Pets

Miki and Stuart are both dog owners. Having pets is wonderful, but sometimes owners have to put up with a lot of naughty behavior from their pets! Listen to their conversation and practice with a partner.

Miki	: Cariad is so friendly, I envy you. She rolls over right away and shows her belly as if she's saying "rub my belly!"
Stuart	: My baby loves people. Doesn't Vanilla?
Miki	: He barks, growls, and bites. You know, dachshunds look cute, so everybody says "Wow, cute!" and try to come close to him. I'm scared when small kids run towards him.
Stuart	: He is a boy, and he is pretty big, so, he must be kind of rough, I guess?
Miki	: Once he bit my son's home room teacher on his leg, when he visited us at home.
Stuart	: Wow, well done!
Miki	: No, no, it was awful! He was really a good teacher. I felt so sorry for him. Also, my dog ran after a girl who then fell down and grazed the skin on her knees. I brought her a box of sweets to apologize, but this sort of thing has happened to me several times.
Stuart	: Hmm... Well, have you ever attended a dog-training class? At first, my baby barked a lot and really was trouble. After getting some training she behaves much better.

Miki : Really?

Stuart : Our trainer is very good. She first visits the dog at home to see what the problem is. Going through the basic training really helps owners as well as their dogs get on with each other much better.

Miki : I think I'd better consult with her. Could you introduce me to her?

Stuart : Sure! I'll let you have her number later.

Build Your Vocabulary

Match the words, then say them out loud.

1. Personality traits

忠実な • • affectionate   こわがりの • • shy

愛情深い • • loyal   遊び好きな • • playful

賢い • • clever   凶暴な • • ferocious

よくしつけられた • • gentle   攻撃的な • • easy-going

おとなしい • • well-trained   よく吠える • • aggressive

活動的な • • energetic   マイペース • • barks a lot

2. Appearance

かっこいい • • gorgeous   垂れ耳 • • long muzzle

優雅な • • furry   立ち耳 • • upright ears

ふわふわの • • cool   鼻先が長い • • floppy ears

長毛の • • silky hair/feathers   筋肉質 • • curly tail

つやつやの毛／羽 • • long-coated   巻いたしっぽ • • muscular body

細身 • • skinny   短い嘴 • • short bill

Free Talk Do you or have you had any pets, or do any of your friends have pets? Use the terms above to describe personality and appearance traits.

Grammar Tips

自動詞と他動詞 **Intransitive Verbs and Transitive Verbs**

Verbs can be divided into two groups: **Intransitive Verbs** and **Transitive Verbs**.

Let's get a clear understanding on the usage for these two types!

Please note there are verbs that are both intransitive and transitive.

自動詞 (Vi) : Intransitive Verbs

Intransitive verbs (自動詞) are verbs which **do not require objects** (目的語).

   e.g. bark, growl, bite, say, run

        a) He barks.   b) Small children run.

When you want to include an object in a sentence, you need to use a **preposition** (前置詞) followed by a noun.

        a') He barks **at** people.   b') Small children run **towards** him.

Make a couple of simple sentences using the verbs below.

   1. look   _____

   2. smile   _____

他動詞 (Vt) : Transitive Verbs

Transitive verbs **are followed by one or two objects** (目的語), **without a preposition** (前置詞).

1) 目的語をひとつだけとる他動詞 (単一他動詞 Monotransitive Verb)

   e.g. rub, love, bite, graze, attend, visit, help, introduce

        a) She loves people.   b) I attended a dog-training class.

   Make a couple of simple sentences using the verbs below.

   1. help   _____

   2. visit   _____

2) 目的語を2つとる他動詞 (二重他動詞 Ditransitive Verb)

   e.g. bring, show, hand, give, send

        a) I brought her a box of sweets.   b) He showed me a picture.

   Make a couple of simple sentences using the verbs below.

   1. give   _____

   2. tell   _____

Let's Discuss

Do you agree or disagree with the opinions below? What do you think?

1. For me, having pets is a terrible idea. I really love being free. If you have pets, you have to give up traveling and you can't go out all day. Oh, keeping pets also costs you a lot; vaccinations, food, cages, etc. I'd rather spend money on a date.

2. People think of having pets as easy. Most people just want to satisfy their material desires and close their eyes to what's happening behind the pet business or public health centers. Animals shouldn't be bought and sold for commercial purposes, like toys.

3. Animals heal people, like the therapy dogs at nursing homes. People tell lies, betray you and judge you by your appearance or what you have. But animals are genuine. Once they join your family, they love you forever, and they never doubt your affection.

Questions

Work with a partner. Ask and answer the questions in turn. When answering, add some extra information related to the question.

1. Have you ever had any animals other than dogs or cats, for example a goat, sheep, chickens, etc.?

2. Have you ever heard of any difficulties related to pets in your neighborhood? How were these problems tackled? Were there any positive outcomes?

3. In recent times, Nishikigoi ornamental carp have become very popular in foreign countries. Export of such carp is said to equal export sales for rice. Have you or your relatives ever had a pond with ornamental carp?

4. Do you think it is a good idea to keep tropical fish or jellyfish in a tank at home?

5. In your view, is it acceptable to keep unusual pets such as insects or reptiles?

6. What's your dream pet?

Quick Decision-Making Game

Work with a partner. You are required to show whether you are for or against the statements. You are given a limited amount of time for each round.

Round 1	30 seconds

Please try to respond as quickly as possible, replying only "I agree" or "I disagree". Cover all of the five statements in 30 seconds.

Partner A talks to Partner B
1. Human beings are scarier than ghosts.
2. It's better to live separately from your partner's parents.
3. Health is the most important thing in life.
4. Aliens exist.
5. *Yakitori* are always yummy with salt seasoning.

Partner B talks to Partner A
1. Money is the most important thing in life.
2. Ghosts do not exist.
3. The best meat for a curry is chicken.
4. People should sleep more than seven hours a day to be healthy.
5. A tip for a successful relationship with your partner is not to tell the truth.

Round 2
2 minutes

Please try to respond as quickly as possible, replying "I agree" or "I disagree". Then add one or more sentences to support your standpoint. Cover all of the three statements in 2 minutes.

Partner A talks to Partner B

1. It is good for children to play video games to acquire computer skills.
2. People who say "I'm always right" are mostly wrong.
3. When the traffic signal is yellow, you should increase your speed to cross the intersection.

Partner B talks to Partner A

1. When you are on an escalator, you should keep to the right side.
2. Human beings are harmful to the Earth.
3. Whenever you are in a rush, all the traffic signals turn red.

Round 3
3 minutes

Please try to respond as quickly as possible, replying "I agree" or "I disagree". Then add one or more sentences to support your standpoint. Cover all of the three statements in 3 minutes.

Partner A talks to Partner B

1. The Japanese government should spend more money on the welfare of elderly people.
2. We need to give up mass consumption to stop food waste.
3. The Internet is an excellent tool to share information.

Partner B talks to Partner A

1. The Japanese government should spend more money to support families with young children.
2. Animals shouldn't be sold at pet shops.
3. We have to give up using plastics and PET bottles to protect our environment.

Kent and his family have been staying in Cairns for their vacation. Now he is calling a travel agency to book a tour to the Great Barrier Reef. Listen to the dialogue and practice with a partner.

Clerk : Grand Marine Tour. May I help you?

Kent : Hello, I saw your website and I was wondering if I could make a reservation for the Great Barrier Reef tour from Cairns.

Clerk : Certainly. Now let me check the availability. For how many people and when would you like to go?

Kent : Two adults and a boy, a high school student, 18 years old. Next week, August 20th would be good for us.

Clerk : A high school student counts as an adult, so for three adults... There are two packages we can offer you;
- a scenic helicopter flight to tour Green Island,
- or a Green Island and Pontoon Cruise Tour.

Kent : I think there is a package to fly to both Green Island and Pontoon by helicopter.

Clerk : I'm afraid that one's fully booked.

Kent : Too bad. We were really looking forward to viewing the reef from the

sky.

Clerk : In that case, you can take a scenic flight from Pontoon. $180 per person, and there are still seats available.

Kent : Sounds great. Could you please book them for us? The meal and snorkeling are included in the fee, aren't they?

Clerk : Yes, they are. You can enjoy snorkeling and a buffet lunch both at Pontoon. Well, then, may I have the names and ages of the persons who are to join in the tour, please?

Build Your Vocabulary

Match the words, then say them out loud.

旅行代理店 ●   ● book   キャンセル料 ●   ● whirlwind tour

予約する ●   ● travel agency   弾丸旅行 ●   ● travel solo

一泊二日 ●   ● Itinerary   おひとり様旅行 ●   ● change flights

日程表 ●   ● one night two days   飛行機を乗り換える ●   ● cancellation fee

通路側席 ●   ● discount ticket   往復 ●   ● tour conductor

格安チケット ●   ● boarding pass   添乗員 ●   ● round trip

搭乗券 ●   ● national treasure   宿泊施設 ●   ● Japanese speaking guide

国宝 ●   ● isle seat   日本語ガイド ●   ● accommodation

Questions

Work with a partner. Take turns asking and answering the questions. When answering, give your partner some extra information related to the question.

1. Do you arrange your trips yourself, or go for package tours organized through a travel agency?
2. Do you enjoy traveling solo?
3. Do you use the Internet to buy travel tickets or make reservations? Which website do you use the most?
4. Which do you prefer, traveling abroad or in Japan?
5. What type of transportation do you like to take when traveling?
6. Would you like to have a cruise on a luxury liner? Or, have you ever done that?
7. Do you enjoy talking to locals in English when you go on trips abroad?
8. Have you ever visited World Heritage Sites in Japan, such as Horyuji temple, Himeji castle, Yakushima island, the Shirakami-Sanchi mountain range, etc.?
9. Have you ever visited World Heritage Sites in foreign countries, such as Machu-Pichu, the Roman Colosseum, Stonehenge, Angkor Wat, etc.?
10. Have you ever visited any of the Japan Heritage sites designated by the Japanese government?

Exercise
Let's Guess

World Heritage Site Ranking

Here is a ranking table indicating the number of world heritage sites per country. Guess the top five countries and use the table on the right to fill in the blanks. Also, where would you place Japan in the rankings?

Ranking	Country	Number of sites
1		55
1		55
3		48
4		46
5		45
⋮	⋮	⋮
( )	Japan	23

Germany
Italy
China
France
Mexico
Russia
U.S.A
Spain
U.K.

Exercise
Make a Dialogue

Work with a partner. Partner A is a customer making a call to a travel agency to arrange a travel plan. Here is a table to help your planning. Partner B is a clerk serving Partner A, to help him/her book hotel rooms and optional attractions. Then change roles.

Package tour destination	Days	From	Number of tourist(s)	Room type	Option
Okinawa	2 days	April 23	1	single	City tour
Hokkaido	3 days	July 20	2	double	Mountain hike with a guide
Taiwan	5 days	Sept 15	3	twin	Marine sports
Vietnam	7 days	Nov 7	4	family suite	Food, wine and nightlife
Hawaii	10 days	Dec 27	5		Local craft class

Clues to structure your conversation

Customer

- I was wondering if …
- Could I make a reservation for…?
- Could you please book … for me?
- I'd like to take

Clerk

- May I ask for how many people?
- When would you like to …?
- I'll check the availability.
- May I have names and ages of the participants?

51

Unit 11 Injury / Sports

Sachiko is someone who absolutely loves sports. She especially enjoys the track and field held at the Masters Athletics meets. As a big meet approached, Sachiko practiced so hard that she developed a problem with her foot. Listen to the dialogue between Sachiko and the doctor, then practice with a partner.

Doctor : This letter of introduction says, "bone fracture appeared to occur in the process of standing up". Could you please describe what happened?

Sachiko : I was sitting on the tatami-mat floor, and when I stood up, I felt something snap in my right foot.

Doctor : Hmm, it snapped... Do you have any idea why this might have happened?

Sachiko : I go running sometimes during the week, short distance races. That could be the cause, I guess.

Doctor : Let's carry out a CT scan to see whether there are any other problems, like tumors in the bone for example.

Doctor : The scan doesn't suggest any possible cause of fracture, so it must be a stress fracture. There are two kinds of treatment to choose from: conservative therapy or surgery. If you don't do active sports, we would go for conservative therapy.

Sachiko : Doctor, I need to fix it quickly. I'm joining in the Masters Athletics national meet at the end of this month.

Doctor : This month? That'd be difficult. You should give it three months before you resume practice.

Sachiko : Oh, no. I'm aiming to break the meet record this year. Plus, I'm planning to participate in the Asian meet next fall.

Doctor : You may need to give up the national meet. So, with this in mind, let's use a bolt to connect the fractured bone, this is probably the best way to treat it. Sport will have to wait until next spring, but you should have enough time to prepare for the autumn meet.

Sachiko : Say doctor, if I undergo the surgery, could you please make it super good to allow me to run much faster? I can pay you good money!

Doctor : Ahem. I don't know about that...

Build Your Vocabulary

Match the words, then say them out loud.

頭にこぶができる •　　　• bruise one's forehead

額に青あざをつくる •　　　• get a bump on one's head

首の筋を違える •　　　• break one's arm

むち打ちになる •　　　• get a crick in one's neck

腕を骨折する •　　　• get whiplash

ひじを擦りむく •　　　• injure one's leg

ぎっくり腰になる •　　　• hurt a leg muscle

足をケガする •　　　• strain one's back

腿に肉ばなれをおこす •　　　• scrape one's elbow

足の筋を痛める •　　　• pull a muscle in one's thigh

Imagine

Suppose you had an operation two days ago and have been hospitalized. You are annoyed because a fellow patient in your room talks loudly from the moment they wake up, watches TV all day without earphones, snores loudly and passes wind a lot. Would you complain to them?

Questions

Injury
Work with a partner. Take turns asking and answering the questions. When answering, give your partner some extra information other than yes or no.

1. Have you ever had an injury while doing sports? How did it happen?
2. How many times have you broken a bone?
3. How often have you had a bruise?
4. What's the best way to prevent injuries?
5. Doctors say appropriate exercise is essential to stay in shape. What do you think about that?
6. If you had to have plastic surgery for a broken bone, or a slipped or herniated disk, which medical institution in your area would you choose?

Expressions

Make sentences using a combination of the words given below.

"must be" ～にちがいない

Example: It must be a stress fracture.

she / tired	they / aliens	the dog / hungry	it / difficult	it / fun

he / police officer	you / kidding	the guy / famous artist	that / true

"物／事 + have to wait" ～まで待たないといけない

Example: The party has to wait until his recovery.

your birthday party / Friday	Disneyland / the exam is finished

Japan's modernization / the Meiji restoration was implemented

Questions

Sports

Work with a partner to take turns asking and answering the questions below. When answering, try to give your partner some extra information.

1. Do you walk a lot? How many steps do you walk a day?
2. Do you do any sports or exercise? How often?
3. Can you swim? Which is your favorite swimming style - crawl, breaststroke, back stroke, butterfly or dog paddle?
4. How many meters can you swim?
5. Did you belong to any sports clubs when you were in junior high or high school?
6. Have you ever won any medals or testimonials in sport?
7. Which sport is the most exciting to watch on TV?
8. How long can you watch a sports game on TV?
9. Some people like team games, others prefer individual games. Which type of games do you prefer?
10. What are the merits of doing sports?

Unit 12 Friends

Maria and Shinya have been team-mates in a soft volleyball circle for years. After practice, they usually chat a lot about all the things going on in their daily lives. Listen to their conversation and practice with a partner.

Maria   : I feel so refreshed after a game!

Shinya   : That's the secret of a healthy life. Phew, now I'm starving.

Maria   : Hey, Shinya, last week I met some of my old girl friends. They were so caring and supportive. I've lived all these years and now, more than ever, I am really grateful to have the friends I have!

Shinya   : I can see you enjoyed catching up with them. I tell you, you have good friends, because you deserve to have such friends.

Maria   : Nice of you to say so, Shinya. I've known some of my friends since we were young, for more than half a century!

Shinya   : Years ago, we had a reunion to celebrate the 30th anniversary of graduation from high school. After the event, we started to get together, enjoying a two-day trip once a year. I've really started to enjoy it over the last few years.

Maria   : Back in high school you weren't so close, were you?

Shinya   : No. I guess new relationships formed after we became reacquainted as

adults.

Maria : I agree. Given that there are so many people in the world, and we don't meet or speak to most of them, I think it's fate that brings people together again at just the right time.

Shinya : Each of us has lived our lives overcoming hardships, so I think now we can be more thoughtful about others than we were when we were young.

Maria : We're lucky to have people we can call true friends, from the bottom of our hearts, even if only a few!

Shinya : That's right. Maria, let me take this opportunity to say something to you. I am so grateful that you count me as an important friend.

Maria : I know, so am I, Shinya, and oh, what a shame! I'm broke today.

Shinya : Ha-ha! You see through me! I forgot my wallet.

Maria : Obviously. I have been your friend for a long time!

Build Your Vocabulary

Match the words, then say them out loud.

同窓会 •   • colleague/co-worker   40周年 •   • celebrate

クラス会 •   • schoolmate   祝う •   • close friend

集まり •   • class reunion   恩師 •   • 40th anniversary

大学の同級生 •   • school reunion   仲の良い友だち •   • fate

学校時代の同級生 •   • colleague   縁 •   • relationship

同僚 •   • gathering   関係 •   • former teacher

Expressions

Back-channel feedback

Back-channel feedback is a word or expression you throw into conversations. By using back-channel feedback, you can show that you are listening to the speaker, which helps make the conversation go smoother.

I agree.	Obviously.	Bravo!	Oh dear!
That's right.	I see.	Cool!	No way!
Aha!	Really?	Oh!	Oh no.
Makes sense.	What a relief!	Oops.	Gee.
I know.	Okay!	Phew.	Gross.
Absolutely.	Hurray!	Whoa!	Ew!
Exactly.	Wow!	Oh my!	Aw.

Practice with your partner using the expressions below.

1. The summer vacation is starting from tomorrow.   Hooray! / Bravo! / Wow!

2. We are fortunate we have best friends.   That's right. / Okay. / Absolutely.

3. We'd better finish the work this week.   I agree. / Okay. / Oops! / Gee. / Phew!

4. How about frog ice cream?   No way! / Gross. / Ew!

5. I've given up the project.   Oh, no. / Really? / Oh, dear.

6. We'll be late!   Whoa! / Oops! / Gee!

7. This puppy is so cute!   Aw! / Absolutely!

Questions

Work with a partner. Take turns to ask and answer the questions below. When answering, give your partner some extra information related to the question.

1. How many friends do you think you have now?
2. How many best friends do you have now?
3. Are you rather a loner?
4. What do you like to do with your friends?
5. What did you do with your friends when you were in junior high?
6. Do you have friends from elementary school?
7. How often do you have school reunions?
8. What'd be the ideal number of friends a person would have?
9. Do you have friends who always inspire you?
10. Do you think socializing with your friends makes you happy?
11. Have you ever told your friends that they are important to you?

Let's Discuss

Work in groups of three. Discuss the issues below and take notes. Share your ideas with the class.

1. What are some tips to keep good relationships with friends?
2. What are the differences between friends and acquaintances?
3. What makes a true friend?
4. How do you know when a friend is a best friend?

Never Have I Ever Game

To begin, each player has 10 points. As your teacher reads out the statements, please respond by answering with "I have" or "I have never". If your answer is "I have", you lose a point. It might be good idea to use your fingers or keep a record with tally marks. The game is over when one of the players loses all their points. Then, each player choses a topic from the list and tell his / her own story to the class.

Tally Marks

1	2	3	4	5	6	7	8	9	10
I	II	III	IIII	ᚼ	ᚼI	ᚼII	ᚼIII	ᚼIIII	ᚼᚼ

"Never have I ever..."

1. talked in a very friendly way to the wrong person by mistake
2. been late for a date
3. chatted with someone while having trouble remembering their name

4. caught my finger in a door
5. brushed my teeth with face soap
6. shivered naked in a bathroom when putting my foot in a cold bath

7. texted a wrong person complaining about him / her

8. put salt into coffee instead of sugar

9. put a drawing pin on the chair of a classmate

10. jumped up from a chair with a drawing pin stuck in my butt

11. looked for glasses while they were on top of my head

12. eaten another student's pudding when school lunch was served

13. drunk soba noodle soup thinking it was barley tea

14. entered the wrong toilet (e.g. a woman going into the men's toilets)

15. gone out dressed smartly while wearing sandals

Unit 13 / Autumn Colors

Ken and Norika are close cousins who grew up together like siblings. They love visiting scenic spots together. Listen to their conversation and practice with a partner.

Norika : Phew, that traffic jam was terrible, and I was beginning to wonder if we would make it, but we have arrived here finally!

Ken : It took quite a lot of time to find a parking space, too. I think the number of visitors is increasing year by year.

Norika : Well, there's nothing we can do about it. This is the most popular site to see the autumn colors, and it's the perfect autumn day today. Hey, look, the maples are making a lovely tunnel!

Ken : That's right, anyway, for this season, we're in the right place at the right time. The railings on the Taigetsu-kyo bridge are brilliantly red, they make it such a photogenic scene!

Norika : Whoa, the leaves are glowing in the sunshine. Give me a sec. I'm sending a photo to my circle friends with my smartphone. Come on in, let's take a selfie.

Ken : Why not? Say cheese!

Norika : Look at this, this app makes us cuter.

Ken : Hahaha, whatever you say! Boy, the maple trees are stunning, four thousand of them! Korankei valley is beautiful, with such a lovely path along the foot of the mountain, and the waterfront of the Tomoegawa river.

Norika : There is so much nature here. It's only a one-hour drive from central Nagoya, but it feels like another world.

Ken : Oh yes, and I feel like having a *gohei-mochi* rice cake.

Norika : Tee-hee, so do I. We had lunch only a while ago, still there is always room for dessert.

Ken : The sweet miso paste mixed with ground sesame seeds turns golden brown over a charcoal fire. It's irresistible.

Questions

Answer the question below, then share information with the class.

1. Name the famous places in Japan for viewing autumn foliage.
2. Where's the most unforgettable place you've ever visited to see autumn colors?
3. Are there any good places to view autumnal leaves in your neighborhood? Where do you recommend your classmates to visit?
4. Do you enjoy outdoor events with your friends, family, or colleagues?
5. Name the popular autumn attractions in your area.

Expressions

Intensifiers: extremely / really / very / quite / pretty / fairly

Let's use intensifiers to describe exactly "how good" an event was.

The entertainment was **extremely** good.	最高によかった
The entertainment was **really** good.	本当によかった
The entertainment was **very** good.	とてもよかった
The entertainment was good.	よかった
The entertainment was **quite** good.	かなりよかった
The entertainment was **pretty** good.	けっこうよかった
The entertainment was **fairly** good.	まあまあよかった

Time to use the terms you have learned!

1. Think about the last movie you saw. How did you like it?

2. Think of the last sightseeing spot you visited. How did you like it?

3. Think of the last outdoor meal you had, such as barbecue or paella. How did you like it?

4. Think of your English teacher. How do you like him / her?
   (*Tip: In this case, "extremely" is recommended for your score.*)

5. Think of a piece of artwork or craftwork you have made recently. How do you like it?

Survey

Let's learn more about our classmates. Ask your classmates the following question: "What does autumn remind you of? Categorize their answers using the table below.

	Art	Appetite	Sports	Leisure	Reading books	Harvest	Others
Tally Mark							
Score							

Is your class artistic, greedy, athletic, studious, playful or something else?

Questions

Work with a partner. Take turns asking and answering the questions. When answering, give your partner some extra information related to the question.

Moon Viewing

1. Does your family have a tradition of holding a moon-viewing celebration in mid-autumn?
2. What offerings do you make to the harvest moon?
3. What do you remember as a child related to moon-viewing?

Chestnut Picking

1. When you were young, did you ever pick wild chestnuts when they were in season?
2. Do you know any chestnut picking sites?
3. How do you eat chestnuts?

New-Harvest Rice

1. Do you enjoy freshly harvested rice? If so, where do you get it?
2. Can you tell the difference between different brands of rice? Which variety is your favorite?
3. What's your favorite way to prepare new crop rice?

New-Harvest Buckwheat

1. Are you a soba eater?
2. Can you tell the difference between this year's soba and soba from last year?
3. How many restaurants do you visit to enjoy new crop soba noodles? Which is the farthest away restaurant you go to each year?
4. Which restaurant is the best in your town to eat soba noodles?

Mikey and Sarah are colleagues in the same section of a company. Listen to their conversation and practice with a partner.

Mikey : How did you like your pilgrimage to Ise Jingu Shrine?

Sarah : It was awesome. I was overwhelmed to see Ise Jingu, the head shrine of all the *jinja* in Japan, such a prestigious place.

Mikey : It's the shrine to honor Amaterasu Omikami who is the highest ranked deity in the Japanese mythology, and because of this it has a deep relationship with the Imperial Household.

Sarah : My knowledge about *jinja* and the spirituality of Japanese people is based on the Dewa Sanzan mountains, but the atmosphere in Ise was totally different.

Mikey : It's like comparing the sun to the moon, the sea to the mountains.

Sarah : Exactly. For me, my impression of the Dewa Sanzan mountains is of the deep history of mountain worship infused with the syncretism of Shinto and Buddhism. On the contrary, in Ise, I felt that the gods of ancient Japanese mythology are as vivid and present now, as ever.

Mikey : I understand what you're saying.

Sarah : Also, I was so impressed to hear that, every single day in the morning,

the priests build a fire and draw water like in the ancient days.

Mikey : Gosh, that would be impossible for me. I'd use a lighter.

Sarah : He-he. I bet you would!

Mikey : For ancient people, "a pilgrimage to Ise once in a lifetime" was a common idea they embraced. And actually my grandparents formed a group called a "*ko*" for people to visit Ise together.

Sarah : Wow, really?

Mikey : Yeah. Villagers used to take some sake and food with them to meet people returning from the pilgrimage at the bus stop at the entrance to the village.

Sarah : So these traditions were practiced locally until very recently!

Build Your Vocabulary

Match the words, then say them out loud.

お伊勢参り • • Shinto　　神話 • • spirituality

神道 • • pilgrimage to Ise Jingu　精神性 • • mythology

仏教 • • Buddhism　　宗教 • • shrine

キリスト教 • • mountain worship　お寺 • • religion

山岳信仰 • • Christianity　　神社 • • temple

神（神道）• • Buddha　　瞑想 • • mindfulness

仏陀 • • god / goddess　坐禅 • • zen meditation

仏像 • • kami　　修行僧 • • monk

男神／女神 • • Buddhist statue　神職／僧侶 • • meditation

神 • • deity　マインドフルネス • • priest

Questions

Work with a partner. Take turns asking and answering the questions. When answering, give your partner some extra information related to the question.

Ise Jingu

1. Have you ever visited Ise Jingu and surrounded areas? What was the most impressive part of it?
2. What do you think is the main purpose of the relocation of shrine buildings ("*Sengu*") every twenty years?
3. Do you know if your ancestors visited Ise Jingu as part of a village pilgrimage group?
4. Do you recommend your friends from foreign countries to visit Ise Jingu?

Historical Religious Sites

1. Not only Japanese but also foreigners love to visit Japan's historical religious sites. What aspects of those sites do you think are particularly attractive for such visitors?
2. Do you visit Buddhist temples and Shinto shrines as a religious pilgrim or as a tourist?
3. Are you a religious or spiritual person?
   (Here "spiritual person" is someone who respects every religion even though he / she doesn't belong to a specific one.)
4. Are there any good places to learn about Japanese spiritual culture in your area?
5. For the first visit of the year, which do you visit, a Buddhist temple, Shinto shrine, church or something else? Why? Why not?
6. Do you celebrate Christmas? How?
7. Do you enjoy Halloween? In what ways?

Survey

Talk with your classmates and exchange information.

Japanese people traditionally visit religious places at auspicious turning points in their lives, such as a shrine-visit *omiya-mairi*, *shichi-go-san* festival, etc. In your area, where do people go for celebrations? Name the special turning points in someone's life and the places they might go to when they mark them.

Turning points	Omiya-mairi Age 0					
Place						

Let's Discuss Work in groups of three. Discuss the issues below and take notes. Share your ideas with the class.

1. Japanese people go to Shinto shrines and Buddhist temples depending on the occasion. Why do we have this unique tradition?
2. Some feel embarrassed that Japanese people will adopt practices and traditions from various religions across the world. What do you think about it?
3. It is said that, in recent times, fewer and fewer young people are becoming involved in a specific religious tradition. Why do you think this is happening?

Unit 15 / Technology in the Future

Ellie and Sam work in the same department in a company. Listen to their conversation and practice with a partner.

Ellie : Hey, Sam, have you heard of avatar robots? They're not an AI thing, but 'another self', like in the movie "Avatar".

Sam : Yeah, I know, it was featured in a TV show a couple of days ago, right? I was surprised at the number of businesses and people that have already started to use these sorts of robots.

Ellie : Even people with severe disabilities or illnesses who are not able to physically turn up to work, can still work as if they were actually there! What an amazing idea!

Sam : The developer said he realized that the key to living meaningfully lies within human instincts and can only really be fulfilled within human relationships.

Ellie : We human beings are social animals, it gives us pleasure to feel we're contributing to society or to have bonds with people. We don't appreciate it so much when we are in good health, though.

Sam : For sure. I respect the guy who developed this a lot, his work will help people to regain a sense of meaning and pleasure in life.

Ellie : Say, Sam, maybe we'll end up being taken care of by avatar robots in the

future.

Sam : I'd rather take care of myself using an avatar if I ever became bedridden.

Ellie : Doesn't that sounds a bit sad...? Hey! Let's take care of each other if that ever happens!

Sam : You take care of me?! Thanks, but I'll pass. I might not be able to rest peacefully in my bed, I can imagine you slapping my butt, saying "Hey cheer up!". Ha-ha!

Build Your Vocabulary

Match the words, then say them out loud.

精神的な • • technology   効果的 • • effective
身体的な • • support / aid   コスト削減 • • reduce
支援 • • mental   減らす • • cost-saving
技術 (機械的) • • physical   増やす • • increase

技術 (人的) • • human-friendly   人件費 • • AI (Artificial Intelligence)
役立つ • • helpful   人工知能 • • labor cost
遠隔操作 • • skill   バーチャルリアリティ • • develop
人にやさしい • • operate remotely   開発 • • VR (Virtual Reality)

Questions

Work with a partner. Take turns asking and answering the questions. When answering, give your partner some extra information other than yes or no.

1. Are you good at learning how to use new electronic devices?
2. Do you use the multiple functions available on computers and smartphones?
3. Do you like to play video games on your smartphone?
4. Are you the sort of person who likes to get the latest technology as soon as it comes out, or do you prefer to wait until it becomes more popular?
5. What do you expect from advanced technologies?

Exercise
VR Trip

Imagine you are at the counter of a VR travel agency. Here are the package tours they offer. Which tour would you like to take?

First Class Journey to France
- First class seat for the flight.
- Paris and Mont Saint-Michel.
- Shopping at luxury stores on the Champs Elysees.

Cycling
- 4D technology animation that makes you think you are actually in a movie.
- Vivid VR imagery which helps to motivate you while you're biking with multiple loads.
- By the end of the VR video, the user has achieved their exercise target.

Hawaii Skydive
- A breath-taking view of the blue ocean and beautiful islands of Hawaii.
- Experienced instructors and luxurious state-of-the-art facilities.
- The exhilarating feeling of free-fall, with no risk of injury.

Let's Discuss

Microtip implanting

Work with a partner. First, each student should think of the advantages and disadvantages of microtip implanting. Then Partner A will argue in support of implanting and Partner B will disagree. Discuss the issue and try to convince your partner, then switch roles.
Here are some suggestions. Add your own ideas.

GPS function | door automatically opens | cashless shopping

password authentication | an operation is required

infectious disease | deterioration with time | hacking

Technology in the future

Do you believe in technology? Will the world of Mighty Atom become reality? How will our society appear in the near future? Discuss in class and share your ideas.

Exercise
Think about it

Ideal technology for an enjoyable life

A. What everyday tasks would you like to delegate to robots or machines? What tasks or jobs would you prefer to be done by people? Or would you rather do them yourself?

> **a.** washing dishes   **b.** folding cleaned and dried clothes
>
> **c.** weeding   **d.** shampooing   **e.** cooking
>
> **f.** washing a car   **g.** walking a dog   **h.** shopping

B. What kinds of robot or advanced technology would you like to have?

1. A treasure hunter which is able to locate any missing items belonging to you, such as glasses, smartphone, keys, wallet, etc.

2. An automated vehicle which runs, flies and sails, free from accidents.

3. A pet robot which requires you to care for it, so preventing you from becoming lazy; this robot would encourage you to walk, talk and exercise, to keep you healthy.

4. A device to manage finances, which takes care of your household economy and gives you an affordable allowance each month.

5. A secretary which takes care of your daily and monthly schedule perfectly. You'll never miss your partner's birthday, which will ensure a peaceful life.

会話文　　日本語スクリプト

Unit 1 ガーデニング／家庭菜園

ダニエル　：ジュンの庭はほんとにきれいだなあ。テラスでティータイムとはとびきり贅沢だねえ。

ジュン　　：うふふ。至福の時間ね。今ちょうど花盛りだからいいところに来たわよ。

ダニエル　：あの紫色の花はなに？

ジュン　　：あれはアンチューサ。ほら、昨年北海道でガーデン巡りしたの、話したでしょう。あのとき富良野で訪ねたガーデンのショップで種を買ったのよ。それがこんなに咲いたの。

ダニエル　：ぼくも植えたいな。種ができたらわけてくれない？

ジュン　　：いいわよ。スモークトゥリーの淡い緑もきれいでしょう。ずいぶん株を増やしたのよ。

ダニエル　：あれって秋になると珊瑚みたいな赤になるやつでしょ。

ジュン　　：そうそう。ねえ、ダニエル、私、いちど本場イギリスのガーデンを見てきたいなって思ってるの。そのうちあなたたちもいっしょに行かない？

ダニエル　：そうだね。薔薇の時期は6月から7月ごろかな。ケイに聞いてみるよ。

ジュン　　：食べて歩けて旅を堪能できるうちにたくさん見ておかなくちゃ！

ダニエル　：ハハハ！ ほんとだね。ツアーがあれば調べてもらえる？

ジュン　　：オーケー。旅行のパンフレットたくさん送られてくるから見ておくわね。

Unit 2 道をたずねる／教える

女の子　　：すみません、英語を話せますか？

ヒロシ　　：ええ、どうしましたか？ 何か困りごとでも？

女の子　　：よかった！ じつは、銀行を探しているんですけど、近くにありますか？

ヒロシ　　：どの銀行でもいいの？ キャッシュコーナーでお金を下ろせればいいのかな？

女の子　　：そうです。

ヒロシ　　：この近くにいくつかありますよ。ドアを出て右へ行くでしょう。コンビニが見えるでしょう。

女の子　　：ちょっと待ってくださいね、ええ、たしかに。

ヒロシ　　：あの信号を右に曲がって、その次の信号を左に曲がると間もなく左手にナイス信用金庫がありますよ。その先の角にもチェリー銀行があります。

女の子　　：もう一度確認させてくださいね。あの信号を右、次の信号を左、ですね。

ヒロシ　　：そうそう。

女の子　　：ありがとう、助かりました。何人かに尋ねてみたんですが英語が通じなくて。

ヒロシ　　：お役に立ててよかった。気を付けて。

女の子　　：ありがとうございました。ではまた。

Unit 3 ガストロノミー

テル　　　：ねえ、「ガストロノミー」って何？ ユネスコの食文化創造都市に、日本で初めて鶴岡市が認定されたって話だけど。

カズオ　　：そうだなあ、美食、って意味で使われもするけど、ガス

トロノミーっていう言葉は、食に関する幅広い分野を含むことができるんだ。

テル　　　：よくわかんないなあ。もう少し砕いて言ってみてくれる？

カズオ　　：ああ。食材そのものだけでなく、地域に根差した伝統食とか、食習慣、漁業方法、農法、その土地のテロワールのような、エコロジーの分野までその概念に入ってくるんだ。

テル　　　：それなら範囲が相当広がるわね。

カズオ　　：分野別に考察してみると、これまで当たり前だったことが、世界から見たらとても独自性のある文化だった、って気づくことがあるんだ。例えばぼくたちにはワイルドガストロノミーがある。

テル　　　：ワイルド？ 私たちすごいもの食べてそう！

カズオ　　：ハハハ！ そうなんだよ。自分たちが畑で作るもの以外に、日本人はよく山や野原で野生の植物を採ったりするだろう。野生動物も食べるよね。

テル　　　：そういえば海藻を食べる習慣は、世界的には珍しいって聞いたことがあるわ。

カズオ　　：ヘルシーでローカロリー。今、世界的に健康志向になっているから、現代のニーズにまさに合致する食材として注目されているんだよ。蜂の子やイナゴなどの昆虫食もあるね。

テル　　　：昆虫食も将来有望なたんぱく源確保の道だと専門家が言ってたわ。私はちょっと遠慮しておきたいけどね。

カズオ　　：ぼくが小学生の頃は、学校の時間中に、クラスメート全員で田んぼに入ってイナゴを獲ったものだったよ。今でも給食にイナゴの佃煮が出る学校があるんだよ。

テル　　　：ほんとに？ うーん……、それはその、興味深いかも……。

Unit 4 お花見

ヨウコ　　：うわあ、満開ですね。いいタイミングで来られてラッキーでしたね。造幣局の夜桜は格別！

タカシ　　：せやろ。八重咲きの桜が多いから、花の色もピンクが深くて、きれいやな。ソメイヨシノを堪能したあとに、また違った趣を楽しめるのがええんや。

ヨウコ　　：これは紅手毬っていうんですね。この枝先、ほんまに丸うてボールがたくさんなってるみたい。うーん、めっちゃいい香り。この立派な古木は楊貴妃ですって。魅惑的なネーミングですね。

タカシ　　：やや、課長せっかちやからどんどん歩いていきよる。この後の飲み会のことしか頭にないんちゃうか。

ヨウコ　　：そりゃそうに決まってますやんか。課長ったら今日はもうお昼からそわそわして、さっさと仕事終わらしてましたもん。

タカシ　　：せっかくみんなで来たのに、愛想ないなあ。花を愛でるために来とるんやないか。

ヨウコ　　：まあ、うちの部署の恒例行事で毎年来てますからね。花より団子、ですよ。しかも部長がいれば、いつもはいけないお店に行けるもの。

タカシ　　：あのな、わしばっかりいっつも奢らなあかんねん。わしの財布、飲み会の後弱りおんねんで。

ヨウコ　　：太っ腹なのが部長のいいところなんですから。こうやって部下にいい思いさせておいたら、いいこともありますって。部長に頼み事されてイヤなんて言う人誰もいませ

んもの。

タカシ　：そかー。あれ、あんた今朝「その仕事私やりません」言うとったで！

ヨウコ　：そうやったっけ？

Unit 5 さし歯が抜けた！

マリー　：やっほー。

ジョー　：あれ、マリー、前歯をどうしたの？

マリー　：ハハハ、さし歯が抜けちゃったの。

ジョー　：ぼくも前に抜けたことある。

マリー　：ほんと？

ジョー　：カナダに旅行した時に、豪勢なランチを食べててね、ロブスターにかぶりついたらぽろっと。

マリー　：ワハハ！　その歯どこ行っちゃったの？

ジョー　：お腹の中！

マリー　：わー、そりゃあ大変だったんじゃない？

ジョー　：それがそうでもなかったんだ。上唇で歯がないとこ隠して、口を小さく開けて笑うようにしてたら誰も気づかなかった！

マリー＆ジョー：ワッハッハー！

ジョー　：君は何食べてるとき歯が取れたの？

マリエ　：孟宗汁なのよ。ぜんぜん歯が抜けたの気づかなかったの。テレビを見てたら、主人がね、歯がなくなってるよ、だって。

ジョー　：じゃあ孟宗筍がマリーさんの歯を取っちゃったんだね。孟宗筍は噛みきれないからね。

マリー　：歯は高いのよー。歯医者さんに抜けた歯を持っていけたら、それを使えるから安くすむのよね。

ジョー　：その通り。じゃあ今後は気をつけましょう、筍とロブスターに！

ジョー＆マリー：ハハハ！

Unit 6 あわてんぼう

ミキ　：まあ、たいへん！　飛行機のチケットぜんぶホテルに忘れてきたみたい。

ダイ　：えーっ！　ほんと？　落ち着いてよく調べてみて。

ミキ　：カバンに入れた記憶がないもの。今朝テーブルで飛行機の時間確かめて、そのままファイルを置いて来ちゃったのよ。コナからホノルル、ホノルルから羽田空港までぜんぶファイルに入ってる。

ダイ　：いそいでホテルに電話しよう。

ミキ　：えーと、携帯はどこかしら。やだ、携帯がなーい！

ダイ　：ミキ、いい、落ち着いて。必ずあるからよく探してごらん。

ミキ　：オーケー、そうよね、落ち着かなくちゃね。あった、携帯があったわ。

ミキ　：あと2キロでコーヒー農園だっていうのに、ホテルへ引き返さなくちゃならないなんて、ほんとに残念。私ったらなんてそそっかしいのかしら。

ダイ　：まあまあ。誰にでもあることだよ。ホテルでチケットを取っておいてくれたんだから、ラッキーだったよ。捨てられていたらどうなったかな。

ミキ　：行きたかったなあ、コーヒー農園。地元の人のおススメだったからきっとおもしろいところだったでしょうね。お土産もそこで調達しようと思ってたんだけどな。

ダイ　：まだ見ていないところがたくさんあるし、また来年来ようよ。君のおごりで。

ミキ　：私のおごり？　本気でいってないわよね。

ダイ　：本気です……。

Unit 7 料理

マルケル　：みんな、今日は2種類のパエリャを作るよ。シーフードのものがよく知られているけど、パエリャはその土地土地で具材や作り方が違うんだ。肉のパエリャも最高に美味しいから、今日は両方とも味わってみてね。

ジュリア　：わあ、このテナガエビすばらしいわね！　イガイにイカね？

マルケル　：そう。肉はチキン。どれも地元の新鮮なものだよ。ぼくたちバスク地方の人間は、地元で採れた食材にこだわっているんだ。

ジュリア　：私たちの国でも「地産地消」という言葉があって、地元で採れたものを地元で消費しようというコンセプトよ。

マルケル　：それなら「キロメトロ・セロ」というフレーズを耳にしたことはある？　農家からキッチンまでゼロキロメートル。近い生産地の食材を使うことで、消費者は新鮮な食材を食べることができて、地元の生産者も守られる。運送に使われる燃料を節約できるし、CO_2対策にもなる。

ジュリア　：なるほど。独自の食文化を大切にする地域には、同じような考えがあるのね。

マルケル　：エビが首を長くしてるぞ。ニンニクを刻んで、トマトはざく切りにしてくれる？　パエリャ用のフライパンを中火にかけてそれを炒めるんだ。

ジュリア　：ストックが温まったわ、マルケル。サフランを入れていいかしら。

マルケル　：いいよ、5分間抽出だよ。フライパンのトマトがペースト状になったらボンバ米を振り入れて、ストックを注ぐ。

ジュリア　：あとは火加減を気をつけなくちゃね。はじめの5分は強火、それから10分弱火にかけて、魚介類を上に並べたら再度強火で火を通す、と。

マルケル　：すばらしい！　ジュリア、ぼくのアシスタントになってよ。さあ、お米が柔らかくなったらできあがりだ。さあ、お米が仕上がるまで、ここからはおいしいチャコリワインを飲みながらおしゃべりしよう。

ジュリア　：わあっ、賛成！

Unit 8 健康

エイジ　：昨日人間ドック受けたんだけどさ、あの胃カメラなんとかなんないかな。

マリナ　：私も苦手。前にひどい目にあったから、最近はずっと鼻から入れてもらうようにしてる。

エイジ　：君はもう受けたの？　ぼくはいつも誕生月に受けることにしてるんだ。

マリナ　：先月受けて、もう結果が返ってきたけど、数値が悪くて。血圧が高いでしょ、血糖値も引っかかっちゃったし、コレステロール値もよくない。

エイジ　：そりゃよくないね。成人病まっしぐらじゃない。精密検査を受けなさいって書いてあったでしょ？

マリナ　：うん、一番気になるのが腎機能なの。昨日内科に結果を持っていったら、専門の病院に行ってくださいって、

紹介状書いてくれたわ。

エイジ　：それは心配だなあ。早めに手当てしておかないと、ひどくなったら大変だよ。

マリナ　：最近疲れやすくて、だるいんだ。一日中眠気があるし。そうそう、慢性胃炎もあるんだ。

エイジ　：君が胃炎？　なんかよく食べてるような気がするけどなあ！

マリナ　：そうよねえ、食欲はあるのよね。

エイジ　：そうか、まあ、食べられるってことはいいと思うよ。食べる人はバイタリティあるからね。

マリナ　：食べることは人生の楽しみだもの。ケーキが食べられなくなったらストレスで死んじゃいそう！

エイジ　：ほらほら。そのケーキが問題なんじゃない？　コレステロールが高いなら食べ物に気を付けないと。青背の魚やオリーブオイルがいいんじゃなかった？

マリナ　：それに食物繊維もね。大好きなケーキが一生食べれるように、きちんと食事をコントロールしなくちゃね。

Unit 9 ペット

ミキ　：キャリアッドは人なつこくていいわね。すぐにごろんと転がって「お腹撫でてぇ」だもんね。

スチュアート：うちの子は人が大好きなんだ。バニラちゃんはそうじゃないの？

ミキ　：吠えるし、唸るし、噛みつくし。ほら、ダックスって見かけが愛らしいから、みんな「かわいいー」って寄って来るのよ。ちっちゃい子なんて危なくて。

スチュアート：男の子だし、体が大きいから気が荒いのかも。

ミキ　：前に家庭訪問に来た息子の担任の先生の足をガブッとやっちゃったことがあるのよ。

スチュアート：お、やるー！

ミキ　：いやいや、そうじゃなくて。すごくいい先生だったのよ。もう申し訳なくて。ほかにも子どもを追いかけて、その子が転んで膝を擦りむいちゃったり。謝りに菓子折りを届けたんだけど、何度同じ目にあったことか。

スチュアート：ふーむ。ねえ、ドッグトレーニング受けたことある？　うちの子も初めは吠えてたいへんだったんだ。でもトレーニングを受けたらずっとましになったよ。

ミキ　：ほんとに？

スチュアート：トレーナーさんがとても上手でさ。初めは家に来てくれて、何で困っているか、みてくれるんだ。基礎的な訓練を受けておくと、飼い主もそうだけど、犬もね、後がすごく楽になるから。

ミキ　：一度相談してみようかな。紹介してくれる？

スチュアート：もちろん。あとで連絡先教えるね。

Unit 10 旅行

ツアーデスク：グランマリンツアーです。ご用件をお伺いします。

ケント　：こんにちは。貴社のホームページを拝見したのですが、ケアンズからのグレートバリアリーフのツアーを予約できますか。

ツアーデスク：かしこまりました。空き状況を見てみます。何名様で、いつのご予定でしたか。

ケント　：大人2人と男の子1人、高校生で18歳です。来週の8月20日がいいのですけれど。

ツアーデスク：高校生ですと大人の扱いになりますので大人3名様ということで。いまご利用になれるものが2コースでし

て、グリーン島へのヘリコプター遊覧飛行コース、グリーン島とポンツーンへのクルーズコースがあります。

ケント　：ヘリコプターでグリーン島とポンツーン両方に行けるコースがあったと思うのですが。

ツアーデスク：あいにくとそちらは予約が一杯になっておりまして。

ケント　：残念だなあ。空からリーフを見たかったんですけどね。

ツアーデスク：それでしたら、ポンツーンでもヘリコプターの遊覧ができますよ。お一人180ドルになりまして、そちらはまだ空きがありますが。

ケント　：それはいいですね。それも予約してもらえますか。食事やシュノーケリングの費用は含まれているのでしたよね。

ツアーデスク：そうです。ポンツーンでのシュノーケリングと、ビュッフェスタイルのランチをお楽しみいただけます。ではツアーに申込みされる方のお名前と年齢をお聞かせいただけますか。

Unit 11 怪我／スポーツ

ドクター　：この紹介状には「立ち上がる時に足の骨が折れた」って書いてありますねえ。どういうことですか。

サチコ　：畳に座ってて、立ち上がったら右足がポキって鳴ったんです。

ドクター　：ポキっとねえ。なにか心当たりはありますか。

サチコ　：陸上の練習を週に何回かしているんです、短距離の。原因はそれかなあと。

ドクター　：ではCTを撮って、ほかに骨の内部に腫瘍などの異常がないか、確認してみましょう。

ドクター　：骨そのものには異常がないようですから、疲労骨折ということになるでしょうね。治療には2つ方法があります。温存治療か手術か。今後激しい運動をしなくていいのだったら温存ですが。

サチコ　：先生、私早く治さないといけないんです。今月末にマスターズ陸上の全国大会があるので。

ドクター　：今月なの？　それはちょっと難しいなあ。運動できるまでは3カ月かかりますから。

サチコ　：えーっ、今年は大会記録狙ってるのに。それに来年の秋にはアジア大会に出る予定で……。

ドクター　：全国大会はあきらめてもらうしかないなあ。じゃあ、そういうことなら、ボルトで離れた骨をつないでしっかり治すことにしましょう。それがいちばんいいでしょうね。運動開始は来年の春になるでしょうが、秋の大会には間に合うからね。

サチコ　：ねえ、先生、どうせやるなら、手術後もっと早く走れるようにお願いします。治療費、はずみますから！

ドクター　：そ、それはどうかなー……。

Unit 12 友だち

マリア　：試合の後ってスカッとしていい気持ち！

シンヤ　：これが健康の秘訣だよね。ふー、腹減ったなあ！

マリア　：あのね、シンヤ、先週末昔からの友だちと会ったんだけど、みんなすごく優しくて、あたたかいというか。この年になってさ、友だちってありがたいものだなあって思ったわ。

シンヤ　：再会して楽しかったみたいだね。いい友だちがいるってことはね、君がその友だちにふさわしいからさ。

マリア ：シンヤってば、いいこといってくれるじゃない。若いころからの友だちなんて、もうつきあいが半世紀よ！

シンヤ ：ぼくは数年前に高校卒業30周年の同窓会があったんだ。それを機会にまた集まって、年に一度、一泊旅行に行くようになったんだ。ここんとこ、それが楽しくてさ。

マリア ：在学中はそんなに仲が良かったわけじゃないでしょう。

シンヤ ：そうなんだ。大人になって再会してから、また新たに関係性を築いていくものだよね。

マリア ：その通り。世界中にこれだけ大勢の人がいて、ほとんどの人とは、知り合うこともなく、言葉を交わすこともないんだもの。この年になって再会した人たちとは、よほどの縁があるんじゃないかな。

シンヤ ：それぞれがさ、人生でいろんなことを乗り越えてきた経験があるから、若い頃よりもさらにお互いを思いやれる気がするね。

マリア ：でも本当に信頼しあえて、ほんの何人かでも心から友だちと呼べる人がいるのは、幸運なことだよね？

シンヤ ：そういうこと。ねえ、マリア、こういうときだから言うけど、君がぼくを大事な友だちって思ってくれてるの、とーっても感謝してる。

マリア ：私もよ、シンヤ。あー、そういえば、残念なことに今日は財布カラだわぁ！

シンヤ ：アハハ、魂胆バレてる！ぼく財布忘れてきたんだよね。

マリア ：見え見え。付き合い長いからね！

Unit 13 秋

ノリカ ：ふーっ、渋滞でどうなることかと思ったけど、たどり着けたわねえ。

ケン ：駐車場待ちにもかなり時間かかったね。年々人出が多くなってるみたいだ。

ノリカ ：しかたないわよ。紅葉の人気スポットで、最高の秋晴れだもの。ほら見て、モミジのトンネルになってるわよ。

ケン ：そうだよな。ベストロケーションにベストシーズンだからなあ。お、待月橋の赤い欄干が映えてていい感じじゃない。

ノリカ ：うわあ、葉っぱに陽ざしがあたって輝いてる。ちょっと待ってくれる？サークルの友だちにスマホで写真送ってあげようっと。自撮りするから一緒に入って。

ケン ：オーケー。はい、チーズ。

ノリカ ：これ見て、このアプリ美人さんに写るのよ。

ケン ：ハハハ、お好きにどうぞ。それにしても4千本のモミジはやっぱり圧巻だなあ。香嵐渓は、山の麓に沿って小道があって、巴川の水辺があるっていうのが魅力だね。

ノリカ ：自然がいっぱいだもの。名古屋市内から一時間なのに、ここまでくると小旅行した気分になれるわ。

ケン ：たしかに。ぼくはここに来るとどうしても五平餅が食べたくなっちゃうな。

ノリカ ：うふふ、じつは私も。さっきお昼を済ませたばかりなのに、おやつは別腹なんだな。

ケン ：すり胡麻のたっぷり入った甘味噌が、炭火で香ばしく焼けてるのを見たら、誰だってたまらないよねえ。

Unit 14 精神文化

マイキー ：お伊勢参りはどうだった？

サラ ：すばらしかったわ。全国の神社の本宗であるということは、あそこまで格式が高いものなのかと感動したわ。

マイキー ：日本の神話における最高神天照大神を祀っているんだし、皇室との結びつきがいちばん深い神社だからね。

サラ ：神社や日本人の信仰に関する私の知識は、出羽三山がベースになっているんだけれど、伊勢はまったく違った雰囲気だったわ。

マイキー ：太陽と月、海と山のコントラストだね。

サラ ：その通り。出羽三山は、神仏習合の色合いが濃い山岳信仰という印象なのよね。それに対して、伊勢には日本の古代神話の神々が脈々と現代に息づいている感じがするの。

マイキー ：なるほど。

サラ ：それからね、印象深かったのは、今でも原始の時代みたいに、神職が毎朝火起こしや水汲みを行っているんですって。

マイキー ：うへー、ぼくには無理だな。ぼくだったらライター使っちゃうな。

サラ ：クスクス。そうでしょうとも。

マイキー ：昔の人は「一生に一度は伊勢参り」という感覚だったそうだね。実際、ぼくの祖父たちも、講を組んで伊勢に行っていたよ。

サラ ：わあ、そうなの？

マイキー ：そして伊勢詣でから戻ってきた人たちを、村の人がお酒や食べ物を持って、村の入り口のバス停まで迎えに行くのが習わしだったな。

サラ ：あなたの地域ではつい最近までそういう習慣が残っていたということね。

Unit 15 未来のテクノロジー

エリ ：ねえねえねえ、サム、分身ロボットって知ってる？AIじゃないのよ、映画のアバターみたいなもうひとりの自分なの。

サム ：ああ、2、3日前テレビで特集していたやつでしょ。思っていたよりも多くの企業や個人レベルですでに導入されてたんで驚いたよ。

エリ ：重度の障害があったり、病気で出社が難しい人でも、まるで本人がそこにいるかのように働けるのよ。すばらしいアイディアだわね！

サム ：開発者は、人間にとって生きがいとは人間本来の欲求のなかにあって、これは他の人間との関わりの中でしか満たされないものだと悟ったといってたね。

エリ ：人間はそもそも社会的な生き物だから、社会で役に立てるという感覚や、他人とつながれることが、じつは根源的な喜びなのね。健康な時は気づかないでいるけれど。

サム ：そうなんだね。彼がすごいのは、多くの人に、生きがいと、生きる喜びを取り戻してあげたことだろうね。

エリ ：ねえ、サム、将来私たちも分身ロボットにお世話になるときがくるかもよ。

サム ：寝たきりになっても自分の分身に自分の面倒を看てもらえたら気が楽だろうなあ。

エリ ：なんだかそれも寂しいわね。そうだ！そうなったらお互いを看ることにしましょうよ。

サム ：君に面倒見てもらうの？ありがたいけど遠慮しとく。おちおち寝ていられなそうだからね。「ほら、しっかりしなさい！」なんてお尻叩かれたりして。ハハハ！

解答

Unit 1 Gardening

Build Your Vocabulary

1. Flowers

向日葵	sunflower
紫陽花	hydrangea
百合	lily
水仙	daffodil
朝顔	morning glory
蘭	orchid
菊	chrysanthemum
秋桜	cosmos
シクラメン	cyclamen
椿	camellia

2. Vegetables

キャベツ	cabbage
レタス	lettuce
きゅうり	cucumber
ほうれん草	spinach
なす	eggplant
ネギ	green onion
玉ねぎ	onion
にら	Chinese chive
大根	Japanese radish
里芋	taro

Free Talk

じょうろで/植物に/水をやる
water/the plants/with a watering can
くわで/畑を/耕す
till/a field/with a hoe
スコップで/穴を/掘る
dig/a hole/with a shovel

鎌で/庭の/草取りをする
weed/a garden/with a sickle
ハサミで/ナスを/収穫する
harvest/an eggplant/with scissors
イチゴに/ネットを/かける
cover/strawberries/with a net

サヤエンドウに/支柱を/立てる
prop up/a snow pea plant/with supports
薔薇に/殺菌剤を/散布する
spray/roses/with fungicide
カボチャに/肥料を/施す
apply/fertilizer/to squash

Unit 2 Asking for / Giving Directions

Exercise: Explain how to get there
1. go straight, end, cross, second, at, see, on your right
2. turn left, intersection, keep walking, the front of, railroad crossing

Build Your Vocabulary

交差点	intersection
踏切	railroad crossing
地下鉄出入口	subway exit
バス停	bus stop
看板・標識	sign
一区画	block
つきあたり	the end of the road
横断歩道	pedestrian crossing
歩道	side walk
国道16号線	National Route 16
弁当屋	lunch box store
ショッピングセンター	shopping mall
ゲームセンター	video arcade
美容院	hair salon
ガソリンスタンド	gas station
警察署	police station
交番	police box
消防署	fire station
市役所	city hall
公民館	community center

Unit 3 Gastronomy

Build Your Vocabulary

昆虫食	eating insects
分子料理	molecular cuisine
精進料理	Shojin ryori
海藻食	eating seaweed
山菜	mountain vegetables
地産地消	local production and consumption
発酵食品	fermented food
食べ歩き好き	foodie

Unit 4 Viewing the Blossoms

Build Your Vocabulary

fantastic, superb, brilliant, marvelous, great, lovely, gorgeous, wonderful, terrific, amazing, impressive, excellent, inspiring, splendid, spectacular, hilarious, attractive

Exercise: Guess what?
1. B
2. F
3. A
4. C
5. D
6. E

Unit 5 My False Tooth Came Out

Build Your Vocabulary

親知らず	wisdom tooth
前/奥歯	front/back tooth
虫歯	tooth decay
歯痛	tooth ache
知覚過敏	hypersensitivity
近眼	shortsighted
老眼	longsighted
老眼鏡	reading glasses
目の充血	bloodshot eyes
乱視	astigmatism
上の/下の歯	upper/lower teeth
入れ歯/さし歯	false tooth
歯茎	gum
歯周病	periodontal disease
口臭	bad breath
目薬	eye drops
疲れ目	eyestrain
白内障	cataract
緑内障	glaucoma
飛蚊症	floaters

Grammar Tips
A. feet, foot, children, tooth, wolves, leaves, lives, halves

B. series, salmon, shellfish, carp, sheep, cows, species, Japanese

Exercise: Think about it!
Advantages: 1, 4, 5, 8
Disadvantages: 2, 3, 6, 7

Unit 6 Silly Me!

Build Your Vocabulary

あわてんぼう	hasty
ぼんやりさん	absent-minded
のんびり屋	easy going
短気	short-tempered
石頭	stubborn
不器用	klutz
心配性	worrier
温厚	mild
世話好き	caring
頑張りや	diligent
礼儀正しい	polite
負けず嫌い	sore looser
前向き	positive
社交的	outgoing

Grammar Tips
read, caught, shut, written, quit, worn, spent, chosen, bought, forgot/forgotten, slept, forgiven, brought, flown

Unit 7 Cooking

Build Your Vocabulary

野菜の煮物	simmered vegetables
鍋物	hot pot
揚げ物	deep fried dish
洋食	Western cuisine
刺身	raw fish
寿司	sushi
牛丼	a bowl of beef over rice
バイキング	buffet
バーベキュー	grilled dish
焼き魚	grilled fish
オーブン料理	oven dish
麺	noodle
野菜の胡麻和え	vegetable with sesame dressing
大根の甘酢和え	Japanese radish dressed with sweetened vinegar

Exercise: Cooking methods
deep-fry, boiled, frozen, sear, simmer, stir-fry, grill, cooled, ferment, bake, steamed

Unit 8 Health

Build Your Vocabulary

身体測定	physical measurement
血圧	blood pressure
心電図	electrocardiogram
視力	visual acuity
聴力	audiometry
呼吸機能	respiratory function
胸部X線	chest X ray

消化管X線	upper gastrointestinal X-ray
消化管内視鏡	upper gastrointestinal endoscopy
腹部超音波	abdominal ultrasound
血液検査	blood test
尿検査	urine test
便検査	stool test
内科検診	physical examination
乳がん検診	breast cancer screening
婦人科検診	gynecological examination
前立腺	prostate examination
C型肝炎	hepatitis C

Unit 9 Pets

Build Your Vocabulary

1. Personality traits

忠実な	loyal
愛情深い	affectionate
賢い	clever
よくしつけられた	well-trained
おとなしい	gentle
活動的な	energetic
こわがりの	shy
遊び好きな	playful
凶暴な	ferocious
攻撃的な	aggressive
よく吠える	barks a lot
マイペース	easy-going

2. Appearance

かっこいい	cool
優雅な	gorgeous
ふわふわの	furry
長毛の	long-coated
つやつやの毛／羽	silky hair/feathers
細身	skinny
垂れ耳	floppy ears
立ち耳	upright ears
鼻先が長い	long muzzle
筋肉質	muscular
巻いたしっぽ	curly tail
短い嘴	short bill

Unit 10 Travel

Build Your Vocabulary

旅行代理店	travel agency
予約する	book
一泊二日	one night two days
日程表	Itinerary
通路側席	isle seat
格安チケット	discount ticket
搭乗券	boarding pass
国宝	national treasure
キャンセル料	cancellation fee
弾丸旅行	whirlwind tour
おひとり様旅行	travel solo
飛行機を乗り換える	change flights
往復	round trip
添乗員	tour conductor
宿泊施設	accommodation
日本語ガイド	Japanese speaking guide

Exercise: Let's Guess

1. Italy, China 3. Spain 4. Germany 5. France
12. Japan (Information as of 2019)

Unit 11 Injury / Sports

Build Your Vocabulary

頭にこぶができる	get a bump on one's head
額に青あざをつくる	bruise one's forehead
首の筋を違える	get a crick in one's neck
むち打ちになる	get whiplash
腕を骨折する	break one's arm
ひじを擦りむく	scrape one's elbow
ぎっくり腰になる	strain one's back
足をケガする	injure one's leg
腿に肉ばなれをおこす	pull a muscle in one's thigh
足の筋を痛める	hurt a leg muscle

Unit 12 Friends

Build Your Vocabulary

同窓会	school reunion
クラス会	class reunion
集まり	gathering
大学の同級生	colleague
学校時代の同級生	schoolmate
同僚	colleague/co-worker
40周年	40th anniversary

祝う	celebrate
恩師	former teacher
仲の良い友だち	close friend
縁	fate
関係	relationship

人工知能	AI(Artificial Intelligence)
バーチャルリアリティ	VR(Virtual Reality)
開発	develop

Unit 14 Culture and Spirituality

Build Your Vocabulary

お伊勢参り	pilgrimage to Ise Jingu
神道	Shinto
仏教	Buddhism
キリスト教	Christianity
山岳信仰	mountain worship
神 (神道)	kami
仏陀	Buddha
仏像	Buddhist statue
男神/女神	god/goddess
神	deity
神話	mythology
精神性	spirituality
宗教	religion
お寺	temple
神社	shrine
瞑想	meditation
坐禅	zen meditation
修行僧	monk
神職/僧侶	priest
マインドフルネス	mindfulness

Unit 15 Technology in the Future

Build Your Vocabulary

精神的な	mental
身体的な	physical
支援	support/aid
技術 (機械的)	technology
技術 (人的)	skill
役立つ	helpful
遠隔操作	operate remotely
人にやさしい	human-friendly
効果的	effective
コスト削減	cost-saving
減らす	reduce
増やす	increase
人件費	labor cost

MOTTO English

A Communication Booster for Japanese Learners
豊かな人生を楽しむ英会話

2020 年 2 月 15 日　初版発行

著　　者／髙野　あき

イラスト／齋藤　美樹
Special Thanks　Stuart Tormad Martin ／ 目崎　泰樹 ／ 髙野　瑛世

発行所　　株式会社　三恵社
　　　　　〒 462-0056 愛知県名古屋市北区中丸町 2-24-1
　　　　　TEL 052-915-5211　FAX 052-915-5019
　　　　　URL http://www.sankeisha.com
ブックデザイン／alcreation